ELEGANT
ENGLISH

ROBERT HARTWELL FISKE

Elegant English. A Vocabula Back Pocket Book.™ Copyright © 2014 Vocabula Communications Company and Robert Hartwell Fiske. First edition. All rights reserved.

Published by Vocabula Books, an imprint of Vocabula Communications Company, 5A Holbrook Court, Rockport, Massachusetts 01966. info@vocabula.com

ISBN: 978-0-9774368-4-2

Library of Congress Control Number: 2014911420

Read *The Vocabula Review* at vocabula.com

Vocabula Books
Rockport, Massachusetts

CONTENTS

Chapter 1

1.1 Uneducated English   1

1.2 Everyday English   8

1.3 Elegant English   14

Chapter 2

2.1 Grammatically Correct English   24

2.2 Uncommon English   29

2.3 Rhetorical English   48

2.3.1 Correction: of One's Words (Metanoia, Correctio)   50

2.3.2 Inclusion: of the Answer to a Question (Hypophora)   52

2.3.3 Inclusion: of a Topic While Refusing to Discuss It (Praeteritio, Occulatio, Paralepsis, Apophasis)   53

2.3.4 Inclusion: of Abusive Comments (Bdelygmia, Abominatio)   54

2.3.5 Inclusion: of Conjunctions
(Polysyndeton)   57

2.3.6 Inversion: of Normal Word Order
(Anastrophe, Hyperbation)   59

2.3.7 Omission: of Conjunctions
(Asyndeton, Brachylogia)   64

2.3.8 Omission: of the End of a
Sentence (Aposiopesis)   67

2.3.9 Omission: of Words or Phrases
(Ellipsis, Zeugma)   70

2.3.10 Omission: of the Answer to a
Question (Erotesis, Erotema,
Rhetorical Question)   74

2.3.11 Omission: of the Answer to a
Question (Aporia, Dubitatio)   75

2.3.12 Omission: of Words so That
One Word Modifies Two or More
Others That Must Be Understood
Differently (Syllepsis)   78

2.3.13 Parallelism: of Words, Phrases,
Clauses, or Sentences Similar in
Structure (Isocolon)   80

2.3.14 Repetition: of a Word, Phrase, Clause, or Sentence (Anaphora, Diacope, Symploce, Epanalepsis, Epistrophe)   87

2.3.15 Repetition: of Initial Consonants (Alliteration)   109

2.3.16 Repetition: of Vowel Sounds in Adjacent Words (Assonance)   112

2.3.17 Repetition: of a Word in a Different Form (Polyptoton)   114

2.3.18 Repetition: of the Final Words of a Phrase, Clause, or Sentence at the Beginning of the Next Phrase, Clause, or Sentence (Anadiplosis)   117

2.3.19 Repetition: of Words in the Opposite Order (Chiasmus, Epanados, Antimetabole)   120

2.3.20 Repetition: of an Idea in Different Words (Congeries, Commoratio)   122

2.3.21 Substitution: of One Grammatical Form for Another (Enallage)   124

2.3.22 Substitution: of One Part of Speech for Another (Antimeria)   125

2.3.23 Substitution: of the Correct Spelling of a Word for a Misspelling of It (Metaplasmus)   126

2.3.24 Substitution: of the Correct Spelling of a Word for a Misspelling of It (Tmesis, Infix)   127

Appendix A

A.1 Inclusion of Punctuation   129

A.2 Omission of Punctuation   130

Appendix B

More Elegant Paragraphs   132

Appendix C

Silence, Language, and Society   150

ELEGANT
ENGLISH

CHAPTER 1

Let us consider the adoption of three categories of usage.

Uneducated English
Everyday English
Elegant English

This scheme is largely an attempt to give recognition to speech and writing that is beyond familiar, or everyday, English — to elegant English. Without such a listing, people may not understand that they can speak and write well, even elegantly.

As the superfluity of uninspired, careless, grammatically incorrect, slang-ridden English makes plain, elegant English is English rarely heard, English seldom seen.

1.1 UNEDUCATED ENGLISH

About uneducated English there is little to say — other than it is a lifeless, indeed, death-inducing, dialect that ought not to be said, much less written. Here are a few examples.

• He knew they *was* out there for 10 to 15 minutes before he *done* anything.

• I *seen* things out there in the world that I never thought I would see.

• My mom is the one that *brung* me up.

• We were a close family; we *done* things together.

• Don't you have family members that you could *of went* to?

• Men have treated me *terrible*.

• I took everything *literate*.

2

• She wasn't being abused about *nothing*.

• We don't go to parties *no* more; we don't go *nowhere*.

• That *don't* matter, I'm still there with you, *ain't* I?

• *Them* fools never should *of went* there.

• I shouldn't have *did* it.

• Let's start over here with the two of *yous*.

• I *gots* a lot of thinking to do.

• If my son was by *hisself* there would've been no witnesses.

• He's *discusting*.

• I'm the one who convinced him *into doing it*.

Abuses of language abound, especially among those who speak

and write uneducated English.

Whereas people who aspire to write and speak the language well still maintain standards of speech and observe distinctions between words, the uneducated, like some juggernaut, massacre and obliterate. They slay nearly all that they say.

alls. • *Alls* I can say is he was a good cop. USE *All.* • *Alls* you hear them talk about is their baby. USE *All.*

anyways. • *Anyways,* I have to go now. USE *Anyway* or DELETE. • You shouldn't be sleeping around when you're married *anyways.* USE *anyway* or DELETE.

being as how. • That's not so bad, *being as how* we didn't even know we would be on the ballot. USE *because, considering (that), given (that), in that,* or *since.*

better (had). • You *better had* do as your father says. USE *had better,*

4

you'd better, ought to, or *should.*

complected. • I'm 5'2", 110 lbs., and very *light-complected.* USE *light-complexioned.*

could of. • I *could of* if I wanted to. USE *could have.*

drownded. • Two men *drownded* when *their boat capsized.* USE *drowned.*

drug. • He *drug* up the past and complained about the argument we had that time. USE *dragged.*

heighth. • She's over 6 feet in *heighth.* USE *height.* • I am the same size as you in *heighth.* USE *height.*

irregardless (of). • Remember to treat all patients with respect and compassion *irregardless of* their health status. USE *despite, irrespective of, no matter what, regardless of,* or *whatever.* • This would have happened *irregardless of* the Chapter 11 decision. USE

5

despite, irrespective of, no matter what, regardless of, or *whatever.*

leastways. • There's no sense of accomplishment, *leastways* not for me. USE *at least.*

most -(i)est. • We want to take this opportunity to humbly express to you our *most sincerest* appreciation for the many expressions of sympathy you have shown us. USE *most sincere* or *sincerest.* • The panel consisted of some of the town's *most lustiest* women. USE *most lusty* or *lustiest.*

not hardly. • I *couldn't hardly* breathe because he had broken my ribs. USE *could hardly.*

nowheres. • He was *nowheres* near their house. USE *nowhere.*

seeing as. • *Seeing as* you're a woman, does the audience respond to you differently? USE *Because, Considering (that), Given (that) In that,* or *Since.*

theirself (*theirselves*). • Irish people I know don't think of *theirselves* as Irish. USE *themselves.*

thusly. • *Thusly,* I feel he was irresponsible and I feel I should tell him. USE *Thus.* • Because this was described as school shootings and *thusly* presented as gender neutral, the gendered nature of the killing and shooting was ignored. USE *thus.*

where at. • Nobody knows *where* the $100 is *at.* DELETE *at.* • I know *where* she is *at.* DELETE *at.* I know *where* he works *at.* DELETE *at.*

with regards to. • Customers are looking for standard-based applications *with regards to* networking. USE *with regard to.* • *With regards to* the paper you gave out recently, I don't want to read about what you have against your opponent but what you are going to do for the city. USE *With regard to.*

Indeed, much uneducated English is everyday English. The language pullulates with people who hover between the uneducated and the everyday.

1.2 EVERYDAY ENGLISH

Everyday English gives rise to ineloquence, and it is precisely this that marks so much of our speech and writing. Whatever the occasion, whether celebratory or funereal, quotidian or uncommon, people speak and write the same everyday words and phrases. No wonder so many of us feel barren or inconsolable: there are few words that inspire us, few words that move us, few words that thrill or overwhelm us. Persuasion has lost much of its sway, conviction, much of its claim.

Everyday English leads to everyday thoughts and commonplace actions; few insights, fewer epiphanies, can be had with everyday language.

Everyday English is marked by a disregard for or an ignorance of the structure of sentences and the meanings of words. Here are a few examples.

alright. • Invisible Circus might not always make sense, and that's *alright.* USE *all right.* • He'll be *alright;* he's got God on his side. USE *all right.*

go. • I *go,* thank you, but not today. USE *told her.* • *He goes,* I've never seen you in one of those. USE *said.*

good. • He did *good* last night. USE *well.* • He helps me to do *good* in school. USE *well.*

graduated. • Even before *graduating* college, Hughes had published two books of poetry. USE *graduating from* or *he was graduated from.* • I *graduated* one of the finest medical schools in the country. USE *graduated from* or *was graduated from.*

like. • There are people doing things *like* we've never seen before. DELETE

9

like. • It's *like* déjà vu all over again. DELETE *like.* • We care *like* you care. USE *as.*

-ly. • The horse looks beautiful, moves *beautiful,* and behaves *beautiful.* USE *beautifully.* • He saw him acting *suspicious.* USE *suspiciously.* • The U.S. came out really *aggressive.* USE *aggressively.*

(my)self. • She told my sister and *myself* that she was pregnant by him. USE *me.* • Richard and *myself* are going to lunch. USE *I.* • Very large people like *yourselves* can eat tiny amounts of food and not lose an ounce. USE *you.* • Let's hope someone comes along, like *myself,* to take his place. USE *me.* • We feel Mr. Roedler's comments do an injustice to collectors like *ourselves* who currently pay $1,500 to $2,000 for radios of this type. USE *us.*

this (these). • I have *this* interest in administration and informatics and was hoping to set up a short elective. USE *an.* • Late at night, when the children are in bed, she has *these* thoughts of revenge. DELETE *these* or USE, for example, *disturbing*. • He has *this* friend whose name sounds very similar to mine. USE *a*. • Men are vulnerable, they can't help themselves; they have *these* feelings that they can't control. DELETE *these* or USE, for example, *powerful*. • I have *this* failing memory. USE *a*.

way. • Our experience tells us that this can look *way* better than in the image posted. USE *much*. • It's *way* more reasonable now for particular event organizers to climb to the top of their niche or category. USE *far*.

what. • I know John-Joe well and I know he can do better than *what* he did. DELETE *what*. • A study of over 9,000 patients revealed that the obesity epidemic is far worse than *what* doctors believe. DELETE *what*. • The location was a lot safer than *what* it seemed. DELETE *what*. • It's worse than *what* I thought. DELETE *what*.

where. • I saw on TV *where* he was awarded a prize. USE *that.* • I read *where* your neighbor was sentenced for soliciting sex. USE *that.* • It is wonderful, although I can see *where* they might have thought it went on too long. USE *that.*

which. • We heard from Commissioner Kelly this morning that the three individuals, at least one of *which* is a U.S. citizen, haven't been identified. USE *whom.* • We spoke to some of her teachers, many of *which* were wearing blue, Christie's favorite color. USE *whom.* • Russian president Vladimir Putin has said that the activists, several of *which* attempted to scale energy giant Gazprom's Prirazlomnaya oil rig in the Barents Sea, broke the law and were seeking publicity. USE *whom.*

who. • You all know exactly *who* I am talking about — which is odd considering that we don't have princes. USE *whom.* • This is a man *who* even Republican cohorts

12

sometimes find disturbing for the way he uses almost anything to his advantage. USE *whom.*

would. • If that *would* happen, what would you do? USE *should.* • What if she *would* embarrass them publicly? USE *were to.*

would have. • What I am sure of is if we *would have* never confronted them, these white kids would have never given in to us. USE *had.* • If I *would have* been Paula, I would not have started a sexual harassment lawsuit. USE *had.* • I wish none of this *would have* ever happened. USE *had.* • I wish that he *would've had* a stronger response two or three years ago. USE *had had.*

Soon, it is clear, we will be a society unable to distinguish one word from another, sense from nonsense, truth from falsehood, good from evil. We will soon utter only mono- and disyllabic words, be entertained only by what pleases our peers, and adore whatever is easy or effortless.

13

Unfamiliar wording and original phrasing will soon sound incoherent or cacophonic to us, while well-known inanities like *have a nice day, what goes around comes around,* and *hope for the best but expect the worst* will serve as our mantras, our maxims, our mottoes.

1.3 Elegant English

We all know far too well how to write everyday English, but few of us know how to write elegant English — English that is expressed with music as well as meaning, style as well as substance. The point of this category is to show that the language can, indeed, be spoken or written with grace and polish — qualities that much contemporary English is bereft of and could benefit from.

So prevalent is everyday English that the person who speaks correctly and uses words deliberately is often thought less well of than the person who speaks solecistically and uses slang unreservedly. Today, fluency is in disfavor. Neither everyday nor even uneducated English seems to offend people quite as much as does elegant English. People neither fume nor flinch when they hear sentences like those illustrated earlier. But let them listen to someone who speaks, or read someone who writes, elegantly, and they may be instantly repelled. Doubtless, well-turned phrases and orotund tones suggest to them a soul unslain.

Even so, it is not classism but clarity, not snobbery but sensibility that users of elegant English prize and wish to promote. Nothing so patently accessible as usage could ever be justly called invidious. As long as we recognize the categories of usage available to us, we can decide whether to speak and write the language well or badly. And we might more readily decide that elegant English is indeed vital were it more widely spoken by our public figures and more often written in our better books.

Countless occasions where elegant English might have been used — indeed, ought to have been used — by a president or politician, an author or other notable, have passed with bland, if not bumbling, speech or writing.

Although the first two categories of usage, uneducated and everyday English, comprise rudimentary structures — a single word misused, or two or three words misplaced — elegant English, often a more rhetorical style, generally requires at least a few, and often many, words, as these examples illustrate.

• Take away but the pomps of death, the disguises and solemn bugbears, the tinsel, and the actings by candle-light, and proper and fantastic ceremonies, the ministrels and the noise-makers, the women and the weepers, the swoonings and the shriekings, the nurses and the physicians, the dark room and the ministers, the kindred and the watchers; and then to die is easy, ready, and quitted from its troublesome circumstances. — Jeremy Taylor, *The Rule and Exercises of Holy Dying*

• A poor relation — is the most irrelevant thing in nature, — a piece of impertinent correspondency, — an odious approximation, — a haunting conscience, — a preposterous shadow, lengthening in the noontide of your prosperity, — an unwelcome remembrancer, — a perpetually recurring mortification, — a drain on your purse, — a more intolerable dun upon your pride, — a drawback upon success, — a rebuke to your rising, — a stain in your blood, — a blot on your scutcheon, — a rent in your garment, — a death's head at your banquet, — Agathocles' pot, — a Mordecai in your gate, — a Lazarus at your door, — a lion in your path, — a frog in your chamber, — a fly in your ointment,

— a mote in your eye, — a triumph
to your enemy, an apology to your
friends, — the one thing not needful,
— the hail in harvest, — the ounce
of sour in a pound of sweet. —
Charles Lamb, *Poor Relations*

• Perhaps her fading mind called up
once more the shadows of the past
to float before it, and retraced, for
the last time, the vanished visions of
that long history — passing back
and back, through the cloud of
years, to older and ever older
memories — to the spring woods at
Osborne, so full of primroses for
Lord Beaconsfield — to Lord
Palmerston's queer clothes and high
demeanour, and Albert's face under
the green lamp, and Albert's first
stag at Balmoral, and Albert in his
blue and silver uniform, and the
Baron coming in through a doorway,
and Lord M. dreaming at Windsor
with the rooks cawing in the elm-
trees, and the Archbishop of
Canterbury on his knees in the
dawn, and the old King's turkey-
cock ejaculations, and Uncle

Leopold's soft voice at Claremont, and Lehzen with the globes, and her mother's feathers sweeping down towards her, and a great old repeater-watch of her father's in its tortoise-shell case, and a yellow rug, and some friendly flounces of sprigged muslin, and the trees and the grass at Kensington. — Lytton Strachey, *Queen Victoria*

• Listen! for if you are not totally callous, if your consciences are not seared, I will speak daggers to your souls, and awake you to all the horrors of guilty recollection. I will follow you with whips and stings through every maze of your unexampled turpitude, and plant thorns under the rose of ministerial approbation. — Edmund Burke, Speech

• As to my old opinions, I am heartily sick of them. I have reason, for they have deceived me sadly. I was taught to think, and I was willing to believe, that genius was not a bawd, that virtue was not a mask, that liberty was not a name, that love had its seat in the human heart. Now I would care little if these words were struck out of the dictionary, or if I had never heard them. They are become to my ears a mockery and a dream. Instead of patriots and friends of freedom, I see nothing but the tyrant and the slave, the people linked with kings to rivet on the chains of despotism and superstition. I see folly join with knavery, and together make up public spirit and public opinions. I see the insolent Tory, the blind Reformer, the coward Whig! If mankind had wished for what is right, they might have had it long ago. — William Hazlitt, *On the Pleasure of Hating*

• Poor Cromwell, — great Cromwell! The inarticulate Prophet; Prophet who could not speak. Rude, confused, struggling to utter himself, with his savage depth, with his wild sincerity; and he looked so strange, among the elegant Euphemisms, dainty little

Falklands, didactic Chillingworths, diplomatic Clarendons! Consider him. An outer hull of chaotic confusion, visions of the Devil, nervous dreams, almost semi-madness; and yet such a clear determinate man's-energy working in the heart of that. A kind of chaotic man. The ray as of pure starlight and fire, working in such an element of boundless hypochondria, unformed black of darkness! And yet withal this hypochondria, what was it but the very greatness of the man? The depth and tenderness of his wild affections: the quantity of sympathy he had with things, — the quantity of insight he would yet get into the heart of things, the mastery he would yet get over things: this was his hypochondria. The man's misery, as man's misery always does, came of his greatness. Samuel Johnson too is that kind of man. Sorrow-stricken, half-distracted; the wide element of mournful black enveloping him, — wide as the world. It is the character of a prophetic man; a man with his whole soul seeing, and struggling to see. — Thomas Carlyle, *Heroes and Hero Worship*

• I confess I love littleness almost in all things. A little, convenient estate, a little cheerful house, a little company, and a very little feast; and, if I were to fall in love again (which is a great passion, and therefore, I hope, I have done with it), it would be, I think, with prettiness, rather than with majestical beauty. — Abraham Cowley, *Of Greatness*

• By the great might of figures (which is no other thing than wisdom speaking eloquently), the orator may lead his hearers which way he lists, and draw them to what affection he will; he may make them to be angry, to be pleased, to laugh, to weep, and lament; to love, to abhor, and loathe; to hope, to fear, to covet; to be satisfied, to envy, to have pity and compassion; to marvel, to believe, to repent; and briefly to be moved with any affection that shall serve best for his purpose. — Henry Peacham, *The Garden of Eloquence*

These examples are full of wit and meaning and style and song; they are elegant. They do not have, nor do they need, the false allure, the empty zest of slang or colloquialisms. Elegant English, as these examples show, is exhilarating; it stirs our thoughts and feelings as ably as everyday English blurs them.

Chapter 2

Elegant English is grammatically correct English, it is uncommon English, it is rhetorical English. It is all three or any one or two.

2.1 Grammatically Correct English

Grammatically correct English adds clarity and sense to a sentence.

Some people — not a few linguists and high-school English teachers among them — believe that words mean whatever we want them to mean, that distinctions between words are scarcely worth observing, that variations in spelling are welcome, that syntax need not be noted, that grammar matters not at all. But if you want to write and speak well, even elegantly, grammar matters mightily. Indeed, the more we ignore words and their meanings, grammar and its intent, the less we understand each other, and the less civil society.[*]

As an illustration of how little we prize and how little we know correct grammar, consider these few quotations from politicians, businesspeople, media personalities, and other celebrities, all of whom we might expect to speak well, if not beautifully, but all of whom, at least in these examples, speak badly. These are unnotable quotes, a collection of solecisms, by well-known people who speak as though they should be unknown.

• We'd like high schools to take the twelfth grade *serious*.

We'd like high schools to take the twelfth grade *seriously*.

---

[*]As not all grammatically correct English is elegant, so all elegant English is not grammatically correct (see sections 2.3.21 and 2.3.22).

• Let's *take a listen* to what he has to say.

Let's *listen* to what he has to say.

• I cannot believe that there would be a breach between Mary and *she*.

I cannot believe that there would be a breach between Mary and *her*.

• When we spend tens of billions of dollars in adventurous wars *like* we are in Afghanistan, and *like* we did in Iraq, we are not investing in our economy.

When we spend tens of billions of dollars in adventurous wars *as* we are in Afghanistan, and *as* we did in Iraq, we are not investing in our economy.

• What we ask from you *going forward* is simple: Just give us your best.

What we ask from you is simple: Just give us your best.

• Yesterday, the president said I needed to watch what I say; I just want to *respond back* if I may.

Yesterday, the president said I needed to watch what I say; I just want to *respond* if I may.

• We could be in the middle of a crisis *like* we were in 2008.

We could be in the middle of a crisis *as* we were in 2008.

• *There's* just too many candidates.

There are just too many candidates.

• I wish he *would've had* a stronger response two or three years ago.

I wish he *had had* a stronger response two or three years ago.

• Girls have a *high rate of concussions as compared to boys.*

Girls have a *higher rate of concussions than boys.*

• And if there is another al Qaeda
attack, it is *just as likely, if not more*,
that it will be in Europe.

And if there is another al Qaeda
attack, it is *just as likely, if not more
than likely*, that it will be in Europe.

• We cannot keep spending *like there
was* no tomorrow.

We cannot keep spending *as if there
were* no tomorrow.

• We could not do this without
people like *yourself*.

We could not do this without people
like *you*.

• I remember riding up the elevator
with *he* and five of his friends.

I remember riding up the elevator
with *him* and five of his friends.

• *The reason* the strike against Syria
didn't happen *is because* we came
up with a better solution.

The reason the strike against Syria didn't happen *is* we came up with a better solution.

• I *graduated* Brooklyn College.

I *graduated from* Brooklyn College.

Pay attention to how people, whether well known or unknown, speak and write, and you'll not likely be impressed by the accuracy or clarity, much less the elegance, of their sentences.

Quite clearly, grammatically correct English is also uncommon English.

2.2 UNCOMMON ENGLISH

Uncommon English adds piquancy and surprise to a sentence.

Unfamiliar wording or phrasing is one of the hallmarks of an elegant sentence. Everyday sentences use the overworked words, the slangy words and colloquial phrases, as well as the poor grammar, we are all woefully accustomed to; elegant sentences use unusual words, original phrases, correct grammar.

The grammatically correct *It is I* is elegant, and the grammatically incorrect *It is me* is not. • *It was her* who spoke to me that way. USE *It was she.* • He knew *it was her,* but she didn't know *it was him.* USE *it was she; it was he.* • If there were ever shoes to kick your heels up in, *these are them.* USE *these are they.*

The ubiquitous *like* is everyday, whereas *as, as if,* and *as though* are elegant. • He felt *like* he had been cheated by the system. USE *as though.* • *Like* I was saying, he didn't know what the circumstances were. USE *As.*

Phrases like *his going, our traveling their marrying, your joining* are elegant. *Him going, us traveling, them marrying, you joining* are everyday. • It's not because of hate that I'm against *them* marrying and raising children. USE *their.* • There is a value in *us* traveling over there. USE *our.* • I knew he had suicidal thoughts before, but I had no fear about *him* going to jail. USE *his.* • We appreciate *you* joining us. USE *your.*

Elegant is *graduated from* or *was graduated from;* everyday is *graduated.* • When I graduated college, I had dreams of becoming an acupuncturist. USE *graduated from* or *was graduated from.*

How come is everyday English, and *how has it come about that* or *how is it that* is elegant. • *How come* you are not supporting my candidacy? USE *How is it that.* • *How come* everyone else is wrong and you are right? USE *How is it that.*

Me neither, that makes two of us, and *you're not the only one* are everyday; *neither do I, no more do I,* and *nor do I* elegant. • I no longer trust her. *You're not the only one.* USE *Neither do I, Nor do I,* or *No more do I.* • I myself know nothing about

31

the subject. *Me neither.* USE *Neither do I, Nor do I,* or *No more do I.*

Likewise or *likewise, I'm sure* is everyday, even uneducated; the alternatives are not. • I'm so happy to have met you. *Likewise, I'm sure.* USE *And I, to have met you,* or *And I, you.* • I enjoy meeting intelligent people. *Likewise.* USE *As do I.*

A lot, very, and *very much* are hopelessly everyday expressions; *enormously, hugely, immensely, mightily, monstrously, prodigiously* are not. • I won't pretend I don't like her; I do — *a lot.* USE *prodigiously.* • We are *very* proud of her. USE *enormously.*

All right, O.K., and *whatever* are everyday, but *(just) as you like, (just) as you please,* and *very well* are elegant. • I think I'll stay here for the night. *O.K.* USE *As you please.* • I'm supposed to say that, not you. *Whatever.* USE *Very well.*

Would have, when *had* is correct, is

32

embarrassingly everyday. In a sentence that states or implies a condition, *had* alone is elegant. • If I *would have* said anything to him, it would have been one of two things. USE *had.* • I probably would have saved myself a lot of grief if I *would have* just accepted my fate. USE *had.* • I wish I *would have* known him. USE *had.*

Phrases like *aren't I? aren't you?* and *wasn't I?* are everyday, but *am I not? are you not?* and *was I not?* are elegant. • *Aren't I* going with you next week? USE *Am I not.* • He was right, *wasn't he?* USE *was he not.*

Everyday are words like *awful, bad, horrible,* and *terrible.* Elegant are words like *abominable, dreadful, frightful, ghastly, hideous, insufferable, intolerable, monstrous, unspeakable,* and *unutterable.* • What a *terrible* place this city of yours is. USE *monstrous.* • This rhubarb pie looks *horrible.* USE *frightful.*

The fact that is everyday, and the largely forgotten *that* elegant. • *The fact that* they declared bankruptcy means little to me. USE *That.* • Yes, *the fact that* she behaved like a child discouraged my wanting to befriend her. USE *that.*

Similarly, *in order that* and *so that* are everyday, but *that* alone is elegant. • We spoke to her sternly *in order that* she might learn from her mistakes. USE *that.* • *In order that* we might profit from our experience, he had us write an essay on what we learned. USE *That.*

Words like *absolutely, definitely,* and *totally* are everyday; *itself* is elegant. • She is *definitely lovely.* USE *loveliness itself.* • Throughout the whole affair, he was *absolutely kind.* USE *kindness itself.*

Extremely, so, terribly, and *very* are everyday; *in the extreme* and *too* are not. • It's *very* lovely. USE *too.* • I found his book *extremely confusing.* USE *confusing in the extreme.*

I don't believe so, I don't think so, and *no (I don't)* are everyday; *I think not* is elegant. • Would you like to walk along with us? Thanks, but *I don't think so.* USE *I think not.* • Do you have any other questions for our guest? *No.* USE *I think not.*

Phrases such as *am I to* are elegant, but *shall I* or *will I* is everyday. • What *will I* do with her? USE *am I to.* • *Will I* never see you again? USE *Am I to.*

Everyday are *(that's) correct, (most) definitely, I agree, (you're) right, sure;* elegant are *exactly so, just so, precisely so, quite right, quite so,* and *yes.* • August is hardly the time to visit Paris. *That's right.* USE *Quite right.* • She is the wisest person I know. *Most definitely.* USE *Exactly so.*

Expressions like *that's correct, you're right,* and *yes, she has* are everyday. Expressions like *I am* and *she has* are elegant. • Is it really your birthday today? *That's right.*

USE *It is.* • Are we there already?
Yes. USE *We are.*

A phrase such as *do you have* is
everyday next to the elegant *have
you.* • *Do I have* time to take a
shower? USE *Have I.* • *Do you have*
anything to drink? USE *Have you.*

An understood *you* is decidedly
everyday; the plainly stated *do* is
not. • We had a little adventure last
night. Oh, *tell* me all about it. USE
do tell. • *Leave* me alone. USE *Do
leave.*

I'll tell you and *let me (lemme) tell
you* are embarrassingly everyday.
Stillness, silence elegant. • The
frigid cold is hard to endure, *let me
tell you.* DELETE *let me tell you.* • *I'll
tell you,* he's no longer a friend of
mine. DELETE *I'll tell you.*

Who, when *whom* is called for, is
everyday; *whom,* when *whom* is
called for, is elegant. • We've lined
up *who* each team is likely to target
if it's able to secure that No. 1

36

overall pick. USE *whom.* • Montreal's university hospital radiation centers will be facing tough new restrictions on *who* they can and can't treat. USE *whom.*

And here, from literature, are some examples of uncommon words and phrases. Note that many of the examples are made elegant because of a nicely placed, seldom used adverb or adjective; others, because of a clever elliptic return; still others, because of atypically correct grammar.

• She's the most *visibly happy* woman I know. — Henry James, *The Portrait of a Lady*

• But I felt *dimly unquiet,* as though some profound but obscure personal wound had been inflicted. — Margaret Drabble, *A Summer Bird-Cage*

• I'm afraid I was very *disagreeable* last night. — Evelyn Waugh, *Scoop*

• He had to decide questions of *appalling difficulty.* — Virginia Woolf, *Mrs. Dalloway*

• *Decidedly*, there was something in his visitor that he liked. — Henry James, *The American*

• Why not? It's *too tempting* — I'll take the risk. — Edith Wharton, *The House of Mirth*

• She *refused it feebly.* — E. M. Forster, *Where Angels Fear to Tread*

• Can there be anything more *abominable*? — Edith Wharton, *The Age of Innocence*

• They are *unspeakably ugly.* — Evelyn Waugh, *Decline and Fall*

• I assure you I haven't a secret to confide to you about her, except that I've never seen a person more *unquenchably radiant.* — Henry James, *The Sacred Fount*

• I'd never have come to you if I'd thought you'd merely think *odious* things of me! — Virginia Woolf, *The Voyage Out*

• You write *uncommonly fast.* — Jane Austen, *Pride and Prejudice*

• His scent for possible mischief was *tolerably keen* .... — Samuel Butler, *The Way of All Flesh*

• Wait till you see it again. It's just *too lovely.* — Henry James, *Washington Square*

• It would be such a *delicious scheme*; and I dare say would hardly cost anything at all. — Jane Austen, *Pride and Prejudice*

• Have you noticed, Catherine, his *frightful* Yorkshire pronunciation? — Emily Brontë, *Wuthering Heights*

• ... his wife's *detestably cherry*, "Time to get up, Georgie-boy." — Sinclair Lewis, *Babbitt*

- Never in my life have I seen such *colossal impertinence.* — E. M. Forster, *Where Angels Fear to Tread*

- Mrs. Archer was a shy woman and *shrank from society.* — Edith Wharton, *The Age of Innocence*

- Hugo had got his two boots gripped by their tongues between his teeth, and was negotiating the passage on hands and feet, his *posterior rising mountainously* into the air. — Iris Murdoch, *Under the Net*

- But really, Brenda, he's such a *dreary young man.* — Evelyn Waugh, *A Handful of Dust*

- He didn't drink, but he had an *ungovernable temper.* ... — Ford Madox Ford, *The Good Soldier*

- I'm *infinitely to blame* for having allowed this situation to arise. — Virginia Woolf, *Night and Day*

• Thank goodness you're a failure —
it's why I so distinguish you!
Anything else today is *too hideous.*
— Henry James, *The Ambassadors*

• – I have nothing to tell.
   – *Nor I.* — Jane Austen, *Sense and
Sensibility*

• – Are you going to live here now?
   – *I am.* — Charlotte Brontë, *Villette*

• – How quiet and secluded we feel
here!
   – *Do we?* — Charlotte Brontë,
Villette

• – I can't catch what he says
myself.
   – *No more can I.* — Henry Green,
Loving

• – Ever play chess?
   – No.
   – *Nor do I.* — Evelyn Waugh, *Scoop*

• – Do you mean the gilt cup?

– I mean the gilt cup. — Henry James, *The Golden Bowl*

- – I missed you.
  – And I you. — Jane Austen, *Mansfield Park*

- – I'm right across from you.
  – So you are. — F. Scott Fitzgerald, *The Great Gatsby*

- – You will be — you'll share my glory.
  – So will you share mine. — Henry James, *The Tragic Muse*

- – Harriet knows nothing.
  – No more do I. — E. M. Forster, *Where Angels Fear to Tread*

- – There was a little misunderstanding that evening, certainly; does she seem unhappy?
  – Not she. — Charlotte Brontë, *Villette*

- – He is a government official?
  – Yes, my darling.

– Of course, *so he is!* — Rebecca West, *The Thinking Reed*

• – But then you spend your time so much more rationally in the country.

– Do I?

– *Do you not?* — Jane Austen, *Northanger Abbey*

• – Not ambitious?

– *No, I think not.* — George Eliot, *Daniel Deronda*

• – May is no month to allow an old lady to travel in.

– *Quite so.* — E. M. Forster, *A Passage to India*

• – I'll pay when I get my wages, said Paul.

– *Just as you please*, said Mr. Levy. — Evelyn Waugh, *Decline and Fall*

• – I love him. I love him like a brother.

– *And he you.* — John Updike,
Couples

• – I have nothing to tell.
  – *Nor I.* — Jane Austen, *Sense and Sensibility*

• – Anyway, I've had the most satisfactory day.
  – *I too.* — Evelyn Waugh, *Officers and Gentlemen*

• – I thought you were discussing the caves.
  – *So I am.* — E. M. Forster, *A Passage to India*

• – I am surprised to find you alone. I thought you had company.
  – *So I have,* the best. — Henry James, *The Portrait of a Lady*

• – Suppose I don't go to Southampton, and come into town this afternoon?
  – No, I don't think this afternoon.
  – *Very well.* — F. Scott Fitzgerald, *The Great Gatsby*

• *It is I who am* blocking the way. — Virginia Woolf, *Mrs. Dalloway*

• And how am I to prevent *his knowing* these horrors? — Edith Wharton, *The Age of Innocence*

• *You feel as I do.* — E. M. Forster, *Howard's End*

• You look tired — *do* sit down. — Edith Wharton, *The House of Mirth*

• *Am I* to be bothered for ever? — E. M. Forster, *A Passage to India*

• And she showed how the question had therefore been only of *their taking* everything as everything came .... — Henry James, *The Golden Bowl*

• *Was it she* who had placed that note in his jacket? — Vladimir Nabokov, *Ada, or Ardor*

• The older boy, *whom* you saw, and *who*, in his way, is a wonder, the older girl, *whom* you must see, and the two youngsters, male and female, *whom* you mustn't. — Henry James, *The Awkward Age*

• *Am I* to understand that now by mutual consent it is coming to an end? — Iris Murdoch, *A Severed Head*

• Was it all a horrible mistake, *my marrying* him? — Sinclair Lewis, *Main Street*

• *It was she* who actually suggested our getting married. — Evelyn Waugh, *Decline and Fall*

• Rachel, *do stop,* you're upsetting me. — Iris Murdoch, *The Black Prince*

• – I suppose there's no doubt they'll have him.
   – *Who* will have *whom*? — Henry James, *The Tragic Muse*

• *It's I* that *am* no good. — Ford Madox Ford, *The Good Soldier*

46

• At last, here was the youth *who* would not bow down to her; *whom*, looking up to him, she could adore. — Max Beerbohm, *Zuleika Dobson*

• But he'll smash me to pieces. ... *What am I to do?* — Ford Madox Ford, *Parade's End*

• He looks *as if he were* undergoing martyrdom. — Henry James, *The Europeans*

• And *it is I,* he said, who not an hour ago complained that I was without hope. *It is I,* who for weeks have been railing at fortune, and saying that though she smiled on others she never smiled on me. — Samuel Butler, *The Way of All Flesh*

• My dear Zuleika, welcome to Oxford! *Have you* no luggage? — Max Beerbohm, *Zuleika Dobson*

• The service was to sing your praises, *was it not?* — Henry James, *The American*

• I am innocent now. *Am I not*, Mr. Sedley? — William Makepeace Thackeray, *Vanity Fair*

• *It was always he*, it seemed to him, who proposed a meeting. *It was always they* who first rose to leave. — Evelyn Waugh, *The Ordeal of Gilbert Pinfold*

• If you can spare the time, *do* take me somewhere for a breath of air. — Edith Wharton, *The House of Mirth*

• It's rather late, and you have to dress, you *had better* lose no time. — Oscar Wilde, *The Picture of Dorian Gray*

Finally, uncommon English sometimes reaches rhetorical heights.

2.3 RHETORICAL ENGLISH

Rhetorical English adds effect and feeling to a sentence.

Rhetorical English is eloquent English; it is effective speaking and writing; it is the use of figures of speech to move or persuade, to emphasize or impress, to clarify or, even, conjure. It is the peak, the pinnacle, the high point of elegant English.

The following pages offer examples of seven rhetorical figures: correction, inclusion, inversion, omission, parallelism, repetition, and substitution.* Not in the least is this list a complete catalogue of figures of speech, of which there are hundreds. And, as you will notice, some of the examples, though listed under one rhetorical figure, clearly illustrate two or more rhetorical figures. Less important than the name of the figure is the song, the sway of the sentence. Listen to that.

---

*Rhetorical figures are of Greek or Latin derivation. The words in parentheses in the section heads on the following pages show some of these classical terms.

2.3.1 CORRECTION: OF ONE'S WORDS (METANOIA, CORRECTIO)

Where a person amends, or corrects, what he says or writes while saying or writing it.

• If you hear anything against your father — anything I mean, except that he's odious and vile — remember it's perfectly false. — Henry James, *The Wings of the Dove*

• By him the whole matter seemed entirely forgotten; and all the rest of his conversation, or rather talk, began and ended with himself and his own concerns. — Jane Austen, *Northanger Abbey*

• All of us have monarchs and sages for kinsmen; nay, angels and archangels for cousins; since in antediluvian days, the sons of God did verily wed with our mothers, the irresistible daughters of Eve. — Herman Melville, *Mardi*

• In my sleep I had dreamed of a … No, it wasn't like that. Let me put it this way: … presiding over the darkness out of which I had loomed there was a figure, a male shape, with an entirely unmanageable aura, containing such things as beauty, terror, love, filth, and above all power. — Martin Amis, *Time's Arrow*

• Felt, seen, heard, not fully felt, most meagerly seen, scarcely heard at all, and still in me, rattling, like a receding footfall, or Count Dracula's swagger. — Edna O'Brien, *Night*

• The year 1880 (Aqua was still alive — somehow, somewhere!) was to prove to be the most retentive and talented one in his long, too long, never too long life. — Vladimir Nabokov, *Ada, or Ardor*

• Then I went back into the house and wrote. It is midnight. The rain is beating on the windows. It was not midnight. It was not raining. — Samuel Beckett, *Molloy*

51

2.3.2 INCLUSION: OF THE ANSWER TO A QUESTION (HYPOPHORA)

Where a person answers the question he has just asked.

• I was born in a ditch, and my mother ran away from me. Do I excuse her for it? No. Have I ever excused her for it? Not I. — Charles Dickens, *Hard Times*

• Do you think, because I am poor, obscure, plain, and little, I am soulless and heartless? You think wrong! — Charlotte Brontë, *Jane Eyre*

• Man measures his strength by his destructiveness. What is his religion? An excuse for hating me. What is his law? An excuse for hanging you. What is his morality? Gentility! An excuse for consuming without producing. What is his art? An excuse for gloating over pictures of slaughter. — George Bernard Shaw, *Man and Superman*

• Now who was this man? This man was Plotinus Plinlimmon. — Herman Melville, *Pierre or The Ambiguities*

2.3.3 INCLUSION: OF A TOPIC WHILE REFUSING TO DISCUSS IT (PRAETERITIO, OCCULATIO, PARALEPSIS, APOPHASIS)

Where a person brings up a topic as he declares he won't discuss it.

• If I didn't know my place, I'd say that you was a foul old fustilugs, and a mannerless old cod. And what's more, I'd tell you what to do with them. If I didn't know my place, I'd wish St Anthony's fire and the quinance and the flux on your nasty old carcase for taking advantage of a girl's lack of education. But I know my place, so I'll say nothing. — Anthony Burgess, *The Eve of Saint Venus*

• We will not speak of all Queequeg's peculiarities here; how he eschewed coffee and hot rolls, and applied his

53

undivided attention to beefsteaks, done rare. — Herman Melville, *Moby Dick*

• The music, the service at the feast, The noble gifts for the great and small, The rich adornment of Theseus's palace ... All these things I do not mention now. — Chaucer, *The Canterbury Tales*

2.3.4 INCLUSION: OF ABUSIVE COMMENTS (BDELYGMIA, ABOMINATIO)

Where a person uses a string of invective.

• "Clusterfist. Slipshod demisemiwit," Sir Benjamin Drayton's swearing was always too literary to be really offensive. "Decerebrated clodpoles, that's all we have. Sense? Sense, you garboil, you ugly lusk, you unsavoury mound of droppings, sense? Have you no sense? Those things," said Sir Benjamin, "are priceless. You tripes, lights, frowsty chitterling. Priceless, do you hear? You

54

chuffcat." — Anthony Burgess, *The Eve of Saint Venus*

• You're a foul one, Mr. Grinch.You're a nasty wasty skunk. Your heart is full of unwashed socks. Your soul is full of gunk, Mr. Grinch.The three words that best describe you, Are as follows, and I quote,"Stink, stank, stunk"! — Dr. Seuss, *How the Grinch Stole Christmas*

• A knave, a rascal, an eater of broken meats; a base, proud, shallow, beggarly, three-suited, hundred-pound, filthy worsted-stocking knave; a lily-livered, action-taking, whoreson, glass-gazing, super-serviceable, finical rogue; one-trunk-inheriting slave; one that wouldst be a bawd in way of good service, and art nothing but the composition of a knave, beggar, coward, pander, and the son and heir to a mongrel bitch: one whom I will beat into clamorous whining if thou deni'st the least syllable of thy addition. — William Shakespeare, *King Lear*

• This sanguine coward, this bedpresser, this horse-back-breaker, this huge hill of flesh. — William Shakespeare, *Henry IV, Part 1*.

• I cannot but conclude the bulk of your natives to be the most pernicious race of little odious vermin that nature ever suffered to crawl upon the surface of the earth. — Jonathan Swift, *Gulliver's Travels*

• And furthermore, let me tell you, young man, that you're a low-down, foul-mouthed, impertinent skunk. — Sinclair Lewis, *Babbitt*

• Nothing exists outside us except a state of mind, he thinks; a desire for solace, for relief, for something outside these miserable pigmies, these feeble, these ugly, these craven men and women. — Virginia Woolf, *Mrs. Dalloway*

• It is clear you have been a great while at sea, to call those sandy-haired coarse-featured pimply short-necked thick-fingered vulgar-minded lubricious blockheads by such a name. Nymphs, forsooth. — Patrick O'Brian, *H.M.S. Surprise*

2.3.5 INCLUSION: OF CONJUNCTIONS (POLYSYNDETON)

Where a person uses more conjunctions than we might expect.

• I'll be as dirty as I please, and I like to be dirty, and I will be dirty! — Emily Brontë, *Wuthering Heights*

• I fumed and sweated and charged and ranted till I was hoarse and sick and frantic and furious; but I never moved him once — I never started a smile or a tear! — Mark Twain, *Sketches Old and New*

• There were frowzy fields, and cow-houses, and dunghills, and dustheaps, and ditches, and gardens, and summer-houses, and carpet-beating grounds, at the very door of the Railway. — Charles Dickens, *Dombey and Son*

• This, dear friends and companions, is my amiable object — to walk with you through the Fair, to examine the shops and the shows there; and that we should all come home after the flare, and the noise, and the gaiety, and be perfectly miserable in private. — William Makepeace Thackeray, *Vanity Fair*

• He was alone and young and wilful and wildhearted, alone amid a waste of wild air and brackish waters and the seaharvest of shells and tangle and veiled grey sunlight. — James Joyce, *A Portrait of an Artist as a Young Man*

• And those noises, and those sighs, and those murmurs, and those innuendoes, and those emanations, and those come-hithers, and those coo-coos issue from me faithfully, like buntings. — Edna O'Brien, *Night*

• When a man is neither well bred, nor well connected, nor handsome, nor clever, nor rich, even Lilia may discard him in time. — E. M. Forster, *Where Angels Fear to Tread*

• For I have neither wit nor words nor worth, action nor utterance nor the power of speech, to stir men's blood. I only speak right on. — William Shakespeare, *Julius Caesar*

• But I go to Hollywood but I go to hospital, but you are first but you are last, but he is tall but she is small, but you stay up but you go down, but we are rich but we are poor, but they find peace but they find ... — Martin Amis, *Yellow Dog*

• She went on like that for blocks, while Sid murmured, and agreed, and prompted, and listened. — Wallace Stegner, *Crossing to Safety*

2.3.6 INVERSION: OF NORMAL WORD ORDER (ANASTROPHE, HYPERBATION)

Where a person inverts the normal order of words.

• ... a good carpenter, Cash is. — William Faulkner, *As I Lay Dying*

• Of what are these things the signs and tokens? — Charlotte Brontë, *Villette*

• To history, to tragedy, to the past, to the future, Mrs. Munt remained equally indifferent. ... — E. M. Forster, *Howard's End*

• On life and death this old man walked. — Herman Melville, *Moby Dick*

• A terrible confession it was. — Virginia Woolf, *Mrs. Dalloway*

• For the title, it was to be supposed, she had married. — Jane Austen, *Sandition*

• An ebon pillar of tradition seemed he, in his garb of old-fashioned cleric. — Max Beerbohm, *Zuleika Dobson*

• That I could love such a person was a revelation and education to me and something of a triumph: it involved a rediscovery of myself. — Iris Murdoch, *A Severed Head*

• But it was natural that he should gradually allow himself to be over-persuaded by Clennam, and should yield. Yield he did. — Charles Dickens, *Little Dorrit*

• Disillusions she did have. — Sinclair Lewis, *Main Street*

• Of whom was he thinking as he stood with his face turned? — Virginia Woolf, *Between the Acts*

• In this conviction my mother had shared, she had been my ally, but now I would no longer discuss it with her. ... — Alice Munro, *Lives of Girls and Women*

• Droll thing life is — that mysterious arrangement of merciless logic for a futile purpose. — Joseph Conrad, *Heart of Darkness*

• Of her experiences in love she would never speak, turning from them with a weariness and distaste which suggested that they had been born of necessity rather than desire. — Lawrence Durrell, *Justine*

• The charm of variety there was not, nor the excitement of incident; but I liked peace so well, and sought stimulus so little, that when the latter came I almost felt it a disturbance .... — Charlotte Brontë, *Villette*

• Emphatically, no killers are we. — Vladimir Nabokov, *Lolita*

• Suffer of course we must, but we know to whom to look in our affliction, and are filled with anxiety rather on your behalf than our own.

— Samuel Butler, *The Way of All Flesh*

• Them, too, darkness covered. — Virginia Woolf, *The Waves*

• To such a remark, there is certainly no reply. — E. M. Forster, *A Passage to India*

• Fortunate are they who are even sufficiently aware of this problem to make the smallest efforts to check this dimming preoccupation. — Iris Murdoch, *The Black Prince*

• Younger than she are happy mothers made. — William Shakespeare, *Romeo and Juliet*

• Woman unendurable: deliver me, ye gods, from being shut up in a ship with such a hornet again. — Herman Melville, *Mardi*

• In the stillness of the night was a faint sound of dripping water, and presently of footsteps going away.

Then stillness unbroken. — Max
Beerbohm, *Zuleika Dobson*

• About his old friend Lucius Lamb,
John often thought sadly. — Iris
Murdoch, *Henry and Cato*

• Him, pawn, no destiny awaits. —
Martin Amis, *Yellow Dog*

• There he was before me, in motley,
as though he had absconded from a
troupe of mimes, enthusiastic,
fabulous. — Joseph Conrad, *Heart
of Darkness*

• Q he was sure of. Q he could
demonstrate. — Virginia Woolf, *To
the Lighthouse*

2.3.7 OMISSION: OF CONJUNCTIONS (ASYNDETON, BRACHYLOGIA)

*Where a person uses fewer
conjunctions than we might expect.*

• All at once we were madly,
clumsily, shamelessly, agonizingly

in love with each other. — Vladimir
Nabokov, *Lolita*

• She debated it, furiously denied it,
reaffirmed it, ridiculed it. — Sinclair
Lewis, *Main Street*

• He looked sleek, clean, agile,
young, a little raffish. — Iris
Murdoch, *A Severed Head*

• She was exasperation, she was
torture. — Vladimir Nabokov, *Ada,
or Ardor*

• The voice of the sea is seductive,
never ceasing, whispering,
clamoring, murmuring, inviting the
soul to wander for a spell in abysses
of solitude. — Kate Chopin, *The
Awakening*

• She was feeling, thinking,
trembling about everything;
agitated, happy, miserable, infinitely
obliged, absolutely angry. — Jane
Austen, *Mansfield Park*

• I haven't any allegiance, any responsibilities, any hatreds, any worries, any prejudices, any passion. — Henry Miller, *Tropic of Cancer*

• Where is the high life, the conspicuous waste, the violence, the kinky sex, the death wish? Where are the suburban infidelities, the promiscuities, the convulsive divorces, the alcohol, the drugs, the lost weekends? Where are the hatreds, the political ambitions, the lust for power? — Wallace Stegner, *Crossing to Safety*

• For God's sake, let us sit upon the ground and tell sad stories of the death of kings; how some have been deposed; some slain in war, some haunted by the ghosts they have deposed; some poison'd by their wives: some sleeping kill'd; … — William Shakespeare, *Richard II*

• My point is that by moving here I had altered deliberately my relationship to the sexual caterwaul, and not because the exhortations or, for that matter, my erections had been effectively weakened by time, but because I couldn't meet the costs of its clamoring anymore, could no longer marshal the wit, the strength, the patience, the illusion, the irony, the ardor, the egoism, the resilience — or the toughness, or the shrewdness, or the falseness, the dissembling, the dual being, the erotic *professionalism* — to deal with its array of misleading and contradictory meanings. — Philip Roth, *The Human Stain*

2.3.8 OMISSION: OF THE END OF A SENTENCE (APOSIOPESIS)

Where a person abruptly fails to finish a sentence.

• "If you are acquainted with Miss Dobson, a direct invitation should be sent to her," said the Duke. "If you are not —" the aposiopesis was icy. — Max Beerbohm, *Zuleika Dobson*

• "When I think of what I was," said Celia, "who I was, what I am, and now dead, on a Sunday afternoon, with the sun singing, and the birds shining, to the voices of the street, then —" — Samuel Becket, *Murphy*

• "Ah, I protest!" Isabel cried with fervour. "If ever there was a woman who made small claims —" — Henry James, *The Portrait of a Lady*

• In such a night to shut me out! Pour on; I will endure, in such a night as this! O Regan, Goneril! your old kind father, whose frank heart gave all, — O, that way madness lies; let me shun that; no more of that. — William Shakespeare, *King Lear*

• Don't talk such utter — It's a question of morals and of — everything. — Iris Murdoch, *The Black Prince*

• Wasn't it rather horrible, a man who could be so soulful and spiritual, now to be so — he balked

68

at her own thoughts and memories: then she added — so bestial? — D. H. Lawrence, *Women in Love*

• "I don't know. I'll have to — " She stopped herself from saying " — to wait until I can ask Dick," and instead finished with: "I'll write and I'll phone you to-morrow." — F. Scott Fitzgerald, *Tender Is the Night*

• No doubt when the appalled soul left the weary body, the panting lungs …. Well, you can't go on with a sentence like that. — Ford Madox Ford, *Parade's End*

• "But you don't really know anything about Willa, Mrs. Renling," I said clumsily. "She doesn't —" I didn't go on, because of all the scorn in her face. — Saul Bellow, *The Adventures of Augie March*

• "You know yourself, Harry, how independent I am by nature. I have always been my own master; had at least always been so, till I met Dorian Gray. Then — but I don't

know how to explain it to you. —
Oscar Wilde, *The Picture of Dorian
Gray*

• He broke into sweat, lost all his
yellow, his heart pounded, the
garret spun round, he could not
speak. When he could he said, in a
voice new to Ticklepenny: "Have fire
in this garret before night or — " He
stopped because he could not go on.
It was an aposiopesis of the purest
kind. — Samuel Beckett, *Murphy*

2.3.9 OMISSION: OF WORDS OR PHRASES (ELLIPSIS, ZEUGMA)

*Where a person leaves out words or
phrases unnecessary to understand
a sentence.*

• He was not our uncle, or
anybody's. — Alice Munro, *Lives of
Girls and Women*

• The greater idiot ever scolds the
lesser. — Herman Melville, *Moby
Dick*

• Time seems endless, ambition vain. — Virginia Woolf, *The Waves*

• I have laid down my plan, and if I am capable of adhering to it my feelings shall be governed and my temper improved. — Jane Austen, *Sense and Sensibility*

• Her hair was silver-tipped, her eyes large and bright. — Muriel Spark, *The Takeover*

• Louise always eats an enormous amount and never puts on an ounce. So do I and neither do I. — Margaret Drabble, *A Summer Bird-Cage*

• His English and French were perfect, impeccable as his manners, graceful and strong as his physique. — Lawrence Durrell, *Mountolive*

• Half the trouble in life is caused by pretending there isn't any. — Edith Wharton, *The House of Mirth*

• Sometimes my left hand sought her right. — Iris Murdoch, *The Black Prince*

• God made food; the devil the cooks. — James Joyce, *Ulysses*

• An engaged woman is always more agreeable than a disengaged. — Jane Austen, *Mansfield Park*

• Some people go to priests; others to poetry; I go to my friends, I to my own heart, I to seek among phrases and fragments something unbroken. ... —Virginia Woolf, *The Waves*

• Meanwhile, Nicholas touched lightly on the imagination of the girls of slender means, and they on his. — Muriel Spark, *The Girls of Slender Means*

• How young she seemed to him, or how old he to her; or what a secret either to the other, in that beginning of the destined interweaving of their stories, matters not here. — Charles Dickens, *Little Dorrit*

72

• That is, I feigned a magnanimity and he a humility which in part we genuinely felt. — Iris Murdoch, *The Black Prince*

• There are a set of religious, or rather moral writers, who teach that virtue is the certain road to happiness, and vice to misery, in this world. — Henry Fielding, *The History of Tom Jones, A Foundling*

• A man does not recover from such devotion of the heart to such a woman! He ought not; he does not. — Jane Austen, *Persuasion*

• There it was, there it is, the place where during the best time of our lives friendship had its home and happiness its headquarters. — Wallace Stegner, *Crossing to Safety*

• Wooed though he had been by almost as many maidens as she by youths, his heart, like hers, had remained cold. — Max Beerbohm, *Zuleika Dobson*

• Our friends — how distant, how mute, how seldom visited and little known. — Virginia Woolf, *The Waves*

• All of old. Nothing else ever. Ever tried. Ever failed. No matter. Try again. Fail again. Fail better. — Samuel Beckett, *Worstward Ho*

2.3.10 OMISSION: OF THE ANSWER TO A QUESTION (EROTESIS, EROTEMA, RHETORICAL QUESTION)

Where a person neither expects nor seeks an answer to a question he has asked.

• Hath not a Jew eyes? Hath not a Jew hands, organs, dimensions, senses, affections, passions? If you prick us, do we not bleed, if you tickle us, do we not laugh? If you poison us, do we not die? — William Shakespeare, *The Merchant of Venice*

• What does God want? Does God want goodness or the choice of goodness? Is a man who chooses the bad perhaps in some way better than a man who has the good imposed upon him? — Anthony Burgess, *A Clockwork Orange*

• Ah! *Vanitas vanitatum!* Which of us is happy in this world? Which of us has his desire? or, having it, is satisfied? — William Makepeace Thackeray, *Vanity Fair*

• Am I an entertainer on salary, required every evening to play an intellectual farce under your stupid noses? Am I a slave, bought and paid for, to crawl on my belly in front of you iders and lay at your feet all that I do and all that I know? Am I a wench in a brothel who is called upon to lift her skirts or take off her chemise at the bidding of the first man in a tailored suit who comes along? — Henry Miller, *Tropic of Cancer*

2.3.11 OMISSION: OF THE ANSWER TO A QUESTION (APORIA, DUBITATIO)

Where a person expresses doubt,
either genuine or feigned, about the
answer to a question.

• To be, or not to be: that is the
question. Whether 'tis nobler in the
mind to suffer the slings and arrows
of outrageous fortune, Or to take
arms against a sea of troubles, and
by opposing end them? To die: to
sleep; no more; and by a sleep to
say we end the heart-ache and the
thousand natural shocks that flesh
is heir to, 'tis a consummation
devoutly to be wish'd. To die, to
sleep; to sleep: perchance to dream:
ay, there's the rub; for in that sleep
of death what dreams may come
when we have shuffled off this
mortal coil, must give us pause:
there's the respect that makes
calamity of so long life; for who
would bear the whips and scorns of
time, the oppressor's wrong, the
proud man's contumely, the pangs
of despised love, the law's delay, the
insolence of office and the spurns
that patient merit of the unworthy
takes, when he himself might his

quietus make with a bare bodkin? who would fardels bear, to grunt and sweat under a weary life, but that the dread of something after death, the undiscover'd country from whose bourn no traveller returns, puzzles the will and makes us rather bear those ills we have than fly to others that we know not of? Thus conscience does make cowards of us all; and thus the native hue of resolution is sicklied o'er with the pale cast of thought, and enterprises of great pith and moment with this regard their currents turn awry, and lose the name of action. — William Shakespeare, *Hamlet*

• Am I no better than a eunuch or is the proper man — the man with the right to existence — a raging stallion forever neighing after his neighbor's womankind? Or are we meant to act on impulse alone? It is all a darkness. — Ford Madox Ford, *The Good Soldier*

• What am I to do, what shall I do, what should I do, in my situation, how proceed? By aporia pure and simple? Or by affirmations and negations invalidated as uttered, sooner or later? — Samuel Beckett, *The Unnamable*

2.3.12 OMISSION: OF WORDS SO THAT ONE WORD MODIFIES TWO OR MORE OTHERS THAT MUST BE UNDERSTOOD DIFFERENTLY (SYLLEPSIS)

Where a person uses a word that modifies two or more other words, all grammatically sound but at least one of which is unexpected or incongruous.

• ... and finally, after rising to his legs to address the company in an eloquent speech, he fell into the barrow, and fast asleep simultaneously. — Charles Dickens, *The Pickwick Papers*

• ... they ... covered themselves with dust and glory. — Mark Twain, *Tom*

Sawyer

• We were partners, not soul mates, two separate people who happened to be sharing a menu and a life. — Amy Tan, *The Hundred Secret Senses*

• They take Bill into custody anyway, mercifully for him as it turns out, since in the hours logically possible for the murder of Lise on that spot Bill is safely in a police cell, equally beyond suspicion and the exercise of his diet. — Muriel Spark, *The Driver's Seat*

• Mr. Gamfield's most sanguine estimate of his finances could not raise them within full five pounds of the desired amount; and, in a species of arithmetical desperation, he was alternately cudgelling his brains and his donkey, when, passing the workhouse, his eyes encountered the bill on the gate. — Charles Dickens, *Oliver Twist*

• I believe that if one man were to

live out his life fully and completely, were to give form to every feeling, expression to every thought, reality to every dream — I believe that the world would gain such a fresh impulse of joy that we would forget all the maladies of mediaevalism. ... — Oscar Wilde, *The Picture of Dorian Gray*

2.3.13 PARALLELISM: OF WORDS, PHRASES, CLAUSES, OR SENTENCES SIMILAR IN STRUCTURE (ISOCOLON)

Where a person uses the same grammatical structure in successive words, phrases, clauses, or sentences.

• She was a woman of mean understanding, little information, and uncertain temper. — Jane Austen, *Pride and Prejudice*

• ... damp is silent, imperceptible, ubiquitous. Damp swells the wood, furs the kettle, rusts the iron, rots the stone. — Virginia Woolf, *Orlando*

• There was in it neither joy nor despair; neither hope nor fear; neither boredom nor satisfaction. — Ford Madox Ford, *The Good Soldier*

• The cataclysm has happened, we are among the ruins, we start to build up new little habitats, to have new little hopes. — D. H. Lawrence, *Lady Chatterley's Lover*

• She liked so little what she had to do, and knew so well what happiness lay on the other side of doing it, that all the morning she was trembling with nervousness. — Rebecca West, *The Thinking Reed*

• She was indispensable to high generation, hated at tea parties, feared in shops, and loved at crises. — Thomas Hardy, *Far from the Madding Crowd*

• She had shown him all — had shown all, poor darling! only to be snubbed by a prig, driven away by a boor, fled from by a fool. — Max Beerbohm, *Zuleika Dobson*

• She lifted her head and looked at me, her face crimson, her lower lip trembling, her eyes vague and terrible. — Iris Murdoch, *The Sea, the Sea*

• Her manners were pronounced to be very bad indeed, a mixture of pride and impertinence; she had no conversation, no style, no taste, no beauty. — Jane Austen, *Pride and Prejudice*

• If rain drops were kisses, I'd send you showers. If hugs were seas, I'd send you oceans. And if love was a person, I'd send you me! — Emily Brontë, *Wuthering Heights*

• I saw on that ivory face the expression of sombre pride, of ruthless power, of craven terror — of an intense and hopeless despair. — Joseph Conrad, *Heart of Darkness*

• The collar buttons disappeared under the bed, the point of the pencil broke, the handle of the razor fell off, the window shade refused to stay down. — Nathanael West, *Miss Lonelyhearts*

• In the beloved nothing is gauche. Every move of the head, every tone of the voice, every laugh or grunt or cough or twitch of the nose is as valuable and revealing as a glimpse of paradise. — Iris Murdoch, *The Black Prince*

• Someone was blundering about, didn't know the boat, probably didn't know about boats at all, couldn't find the hatch. — Penelope Fitzgerald, *Offshore*

• And then another picture came into my mind. Julian Malory, standing by the electric fire, wearing his speckled mackintosh, holding a couple of ping-pong bats and quoting a not very appropriate bit of Keats. — Barbara Pym, *Excellent Women*

• I was so ashamed that such a scene should spring from Chris's peril at the front that I wanted to go out into the garden and sit by the pond until the poor thing had removed her deplorable umbrella, her unpardonable raincoat, her poor frustrated fraud. — Rebecca West, *The Return on the Soldier*

• To cease utterly, to give it all up and not know anything more — this idea was as sweet as a vision of a cool bath in a marble tank, in a darkened chamber, in a hot land. — Henry James, *The Portrait of a Lady*

• A man with no hat, and with broken shoes, and with an old rag tied round his head. A man who had been soaked in water, and smothered in mud, and lamed by stones, and cut by flints, and stung by nettles, and torn by briars; who limped, and shivered, and glared and growled; and whose teeth chattered in his head as he seized me by the chin. — Charles Dickens, *Great Expectations*

• Think of two people, living together day after day, year after year, in this small space, standing elbow to elbow cooking at the same small stove, squeezing past each other on the narrow stairs, shaving in front of the same small bathroom mirror, constantly jogging, jostling, bumping against each other's bodies by mistake or on purpose, sensually, aggressively, awkwardly, impatiently, in rage or in love — think what deep though invisible tracks they must leave, everywhere, behind them! — Christopher Isherwood, *A Single Man*

• By touch we are betrayed and betray others ... an accidental brushing of shoulders or touching of hands ... hands laid on shoulders in a gesture of comfort that lies like a thief, that takes, not gives, that wants, not offers, that awakes, not pacifies. — Wallace Stegner, *Angle of Repose*

• As they realized themselves in varying degrees, few people alive at the time were more delightful, more ingenious, more movingly lovely, and, as it might happen, more savage, than the girls of slender means. — Muriel Spark, *The Girls of Slender Means*

• Armed at all points against the possible disappointments of her life, conscious of the responsibilities of protecting her mother and sister, worried at the gaps in her education, anxious about nuns and antique dealers, she had forgotten for some time the necessity for personal happiness. — Penelope Fitzgerald, *Offshore*

• Besides, with this creed, I can so clearly distinguish between the criminal and his crime; I can so sincerely forgive the first while I abhor the last; with this creed, revenge never worries my heart, degradation never too deeply disgusts me, injustice never crushes me too low. — Charlotte Brontë, *Jane Eyre*

• Unbeloved by his austere colleagues, unknown in local pubs, unregretted by male students, he retired in 1922, after which he resided in Europe. — Vladimir Nabokov, *Ada, or Ardor*

• The flower bloomed and faded. The sun rose and sank. The lover loved and went. — Virginia Woolf, *Orlando*

• I rang his bell nervously, and entered fearfully, and sat down anxiously in the communal country-house-style waiting room. ... — Margaret Drabble, *The Seven Sisters*

• They were not idle sitting there; their laps were full of work — cherries to be stoned, peas to be shelled, apples to be cored. — Alice Munro, *Lives of Girls and Women*

• He was a morose, savage-hearted, bad man: idle and dissolute in his habits; cruel and ferocious in his disposition. — Charles Dickens, *The Pickwick Papers*

2.3.14 REPETITION: OF A WORD, PHRASE, CLAUSE, OR SENTENCE

(ANAPHORA, DIACOPE, SYMPLOCE, EPANALEPSIS, EPISTROPHE)

Where a person repeats the same word, phrase, or clause.

• Talk, talk, talk: the utter and heartbreaking stupidity of words. — William Faulkner, *Mosquitoes*

• Odd, odd, *odd*, was Lenina's verdict on Bernard Marx. — Aldous Huxley, *Brave New World.*

• You appreciate us all — see good in all of us. And all the time you are dead — dead — dead. — E. M. Forster, *Where Angels Fear to Tread*

• London is now veiled, now vanished, now crumbled, now fallen. — Virginia Woolf, *The Waves*

• Mad world, mad kings, mad composition! — William Shakespeare, *King John*

• Many, oh many, many years later he recollected with wonder ... that

moment of total happiness. ... —
Vladimir Nabokov, *Ada, or Ardor*

• And then they should do some
good to the benighted, the most
benighted, the fashionable
benighted; they should perhaps
make them furious — there was
always some good in that. — Henry
James, *The Bostonians*

• His wife had bleached cheeks,
bleached hair, bleached voice, and a
bleached manner. — Sinclair Lewis,
Main Street

• You flock of fools, under this
captain of fools, in the ship of fools!
— Herman Melville, *The Confidence-
Man: His Masquerade*

• All was darkness; all was doubt;
all was confusion. — Virginia Woolf,
Orlando

• And under the sinister splendour
of that sky the sea, blue and
profound, remained still, without a
stir, without a ripple, without a
89

wrinkle — viscous, stagnant, dead.
— Joseph Conrad, *Lord Jim*

• Well, well, well! Stubb knows him
best of all, and Stubb always says
he's queer; says nothing but that
one sufficient little word queer; he's
queer, says Stubb; he's queer —
queer, queer; and keeps dinning it
into Mr. Starbuck all the time —
queer, Sir — queer, queer, very
queer. — Herman Melville, *Moby
Dick*

• I thought, I must get away, I must
get away, I must get away. I
thought, I'm glad Julian doesn't
know about all *that*. I thought,
maybe Priscilla really is better off at
Notting Hill. I thought, perhaps I will
go and see Priscilla after all. — Iris
Murdoch, *The Black Prince*

• She had gone. Mrs. Dalloway had
triumphed. Elizabeth had gone.
Beauty had gone, youth had gone.
— Virginia Woolf, *Mrs. Dalloway*

• I hate to be poor, and we are degradingly poor, offensively poor, miserably poor, beastly poor. — Charles Dickens, *Our Mutual Friend*

• Furiously he snatched up his tube of shaving-cream, furiously he lathered, with a belligerent slapping on the unctuous brush, furiously he raked his plump cheeks with a safety razor. — Sinclair Lewis, *Babbitt*

• Nobody could guess at the relief I might be feeling. Nobody knew of the exhilaration I felt when I realized that I would not have to live with Andrew for the rest of my life. Nobody knew of my secret delight in his public guilt. — Margaret Drabble, *The Seven Sisters*

• What's your road, man? — holyboy road, madman road, rainbow road, guppy road, any road. It's an anywhere road for anybody anyhow. — Jack Kerouac, *On the Road*

• He was abrasive, always slightly teasing, always slightly aggressive, always slightly (I cannot avoid the word) flirting with me. — Iris Murdoch, *The Black Prince*

• She came home by the unvarying route. She knew every house-front, every street-crossing, every billboard, every tree, every dog. She knew every blackened banana-skin and empty cigarette-box in the gutters. She knew every greeting. — Sinclair Lewis, *Main Street*

• And we shall organize them, we shall drill them, we shall marshal them for the victory! We shall bear down the opposition, we shall sweep it before us and Chicago will be ours! *Chicago will be ours!* CHICAGO WILL BE OURS! — Upton Sinclair, *The Jungle*

• I wondered why she was such a mystery, why she didn't fit together, why she was so unpredictable. — Margaret Drabble, *A Summer Bird-*

Cage

• ... then the wind went round to the sou' west and began to pipe up. In two days it blew a gale. *The Judea*, hove to, wallowed on the Atlantic like an old candle-box. It blew day after day: It blew with spite, without interval, without mercy, without rest. — Joseph Conrad, *Youth*

• If I am going to be drowned — if I am going to be drowned — if I am going to be drowned, why, in the name of the seven mad gods, who rule the sea, was I allowed to come thus far and contemplate sand and trees? — Stephen Crane, *The Open Boat*

• I will achieve in my life — heaven grant that it be not long — some gigantic amalgamation between the two discrepancies so hideously apparent to me. Out of my suffering I will do it. I will knock. I will enter. — Virginia Woolf, *The Waves*

• Elmer Gantry was drunk. He was eloquently drunk, lovingly and pugnaciously drunk. — Sinclair Lewis, *Elmer Gantry*

• His shoes looked too large; his sleeve looked too long; his hair looked too limp; his features looked too mean; his exposed throat looked as if a halter would have done it good. — Charles Dickens, *Martin Chuzzlewit*

• She moves and mingles as if with dreamy feet and legs, but quite plainly, from her eyes, her mind is not dreamy as she absorbs each face, each dress, each suit of clothes, all blouses, blue-jeans, each piece of hand-luggage, each voice which will accompany her on the flight now boarding at Gate 14. — Muriel Spark, *The Driver's Seat*

• There was the truth of virginity and the truth of passion, the truth of wealth and of poverty, of thrift and of profligacy, of carelessness and of abandon. — Sherwood

Anderson, *Winesburg, Ohio*

• Any sudden sound, any unexplained footstep, any unfamiliar script on an envelope, made them startle; and for months they never felt secure enough to let themselves go, in complete sleep. — Sinclair Lewis, *It Can't Happen Here*

• I saw on that ivory face the expression of somber pride, of ruthless power, of craven terror — of an intense and hopeless despair. — Joseph Conrad, *Heart of Darkness*

• The memory is sometimes so retentive, so serviceable, so obedient — at others, so bewildered and so weak — and at others again, so tyrannic, so beyond controul! — Jane Austen, *Mansfield Park*

• It is a kind of cupidity, a kind of fear, a kind of envy, a kind of hate. — Iris Murdoch, *The Black Prince*

• The vision of her floundering in the wake of the concentrated helpers and their feeble charge turned my distress into outrage. Not at any of the helpers, not at Charity's willfulness, not at the solidarity of women collaborating in what only they could do as well, while excluding male intrusions. No, at *it*, at fate, at the miserable failure of the law of nature to conform to the dream of man: at what living had done to the woman my life was fused with, what her life had been and was. What she had missed, how much had been kept from her, how little her potential had been realized, how hampered were her affection and willingness and warmth. — Wallace Stegner, *Crossing to Safety*

• Personally of course I regret everything. Not a word, not a deed, not a thought, not a need, not a grief, not a joy, not a girl, not a boy, not a doubt, not a trust, not a scorn, not a lust, not a hope, not a fear, not a smile, not a tear, not a name, not a face, no time, no place, that I do not regret, exceedingly. — Samuel Beckett, *Watt*

96

• I should want to draw it like a Bat for its short sightedness; like a Bantam for its bragging; like a Magpie, for its honesty; like a Peacock, for its vanity; like an Ostrich, for its putting its head in the mud and thinks nobody sees it.
— Charles Dickens, *Martin Chuzzlewit*

• A man who had been in motion since eight o'clock in the morning, and might now have been still, who had been long talking, and might have been silent, who had been in more than one crowd, and might have been alone! — Jane Austen, *Emma*

• I understood him that it was he who was bored, he who had been pursued, he for whom perversity had become a dreadful menace, he, in fine, who pleaded for my intervention. — Henry James, *The Sacred Fount*

• It was the best of times, it was the worst of times, it was the age of

97

wisdom, it was the age of foolishness, it was the epoch of belief, it was the epoch of incredulity, it was the season of Light, it was the season of Darkness, it was the spring of hope, it was the winter of despair, we had everything before us, we had nothing before us, we were all going direct to Heaven, we were all going direct the other way. — Charles Dickens, *A Tale of Two Cities*

• Therefore I am not to be silenced by poverty and sickness, not by hatred and obloquy, by threats and ridicule — not by prison and persecution, if they should come — not by any power that is upon the earth or above the earth, that was, or is, or ever can be created. — Upton Sinclair, *The Jungle*

• So beautiful, so mystical, so bewilderingly alluring, speaking of a mournfulness sweeter and more attractive than all mirthfulness, that face of glorious suffering, that face of touching loveliness, that face was

Pierre's own sister's, that face was Isabel's, that face Pierre had visibly seen, into those same supernatural eyes our Pierre had looked. — Herman Melville, *Pierre or The Ambiguities*

• If the steering-gear did not give way, if the immense volumes of water did not burst the deck in or smash one of the hatches, if the engines did not give up, if way could be kept on the ship against this terrific wind, and she did not bury herself in one of those awful seas, of whose white crests alone, topping high above her bows, he could now and then get a sickening glimpse — then there was a chance of her coming out of it. — Joseph Conrad, *Heart of Darkness*

• For if it is rash to walk into a lion's den unarmed, rash to navigate the Atlantic in a rowing boat, rash to stand on one foot on top of St. Paul's, it is still more rash to go home alone with a poet. — Virginia

Woolf, *Orlando*

• There was shadow in bureau drawers and closets and suitcases, and shadow under houses and trees and stones, and shadow at the back of people's eyes and smiles, and shadow, miles and miles and miles of it, on the night side of the earth. — Sylvia Plath, *The Bell Jar*

• This harsh little man — this pitiless censor — gathers up all your poor scattered sins of vanity, your luckless chiffon of rose-color, your small fringe of a wreath, your small scrap of ribbon, your silly bit of lace, and calls you to account for the lot, and for each item. — Charlotte Brontë, *Villette*

• Everything we shut our eyes to, everything we run away from, everything we deny, denigrate or despise, serves to defeat us in the end. — Henry Miller, *Tropic of Cancer*

• Whenever I find myself growing grim about the mouth; whenever it is a damp, drizzly November in my soul; whenever I find myself involuntarily pausing before coffin warehouses, and bringing up the rear of every funeral I meet; and especially whenever my hypos get such an upper hand of me, that it requires a strong moral principle to prevent me from deliberately stepping into the street, and methodically knocking people's hats off — then, I account it high time to get to sea as soon as I can. — Herman Melville, *Moby Dick*

• If Julia is full of selfish secret career happiness, she conceals it well. If Candida is thinking angrily of her husband, or sadly of her daughter, she conceals it well. If Valeria is worried about her minibus battery and about cancelling hotel bookings and claiming refunds, she conceals it well. If Anaïs wishes she had never embarked with this ill-assorted crew, she conceals it well. If Mrs. Jerrold is longing to get to

101

bed with Hermann Broch, she conceals it well. — Margaret Drabble, *The Seven Sisters*

• In a soft, green valley where a stream ran through close-cropped, spongy pasture and the grass grew down below the stream's edge, and merged there with the water-weed — where a road ran between grass verges and tumbled walls, and the grass merged into moss which spread upwards and over the tumbled stones of the walls, outwards over the pocked metalling and deep ruts of the road; where the ruins of a police barracks, built to command the road through the valley, burnt in the Troubles, had once been white, then black, and now were one green with the grass and the moss and the water-weed; where the smoke of burned turf drifted down from the cabin chimneys and joined the mist that rose from the damp, green earth; where the prints of ass and pig, goose and calf and horse, mingled indifferently with those of barefoot children; where the soft, resentful voices rose and fell in the smoky cabins, merging with the music of the stream and the treading and shifting and munching of the beasts at pasture; where mist and smoke never lifted and the sun never fell direct, and evening came slowly in infinite gradations of shadow; where the priest came seldom because of the rough road and the long climb home to the head of the valley, and no one except the priest ever came from one month's end to another — there stood an inn which was frequented in bygone days by fishermen. — Evelyn Waugh, *Put Out More Flags*

• All that most maddens and torments; all that stirs up the lees of things; all truth with malice in it; all that cracks the sinews and cakes the brain; all the subtle demonisms of life and thought; all evil, to crazy Ahab, were visibly personified, and made practically assailable in Moby Dick. — Herman Melville, *Moby Dick*

• Fathers were ridiculous: his own obstinate one supremely so. And governments were ridiculous: our own wait-and-see sort especially so. And armies were ridiculous, and old buffers of generals altogether, the red-faced Kitchener supremely. Even the war was ridiculous, though it did kill rather a lot of people. — D. H. Lawrence, *Lady Chatterley's Lover*

• They were staggered to learn that a real tangible person, living in Minnesota, and married to their own flesh-and-blood relation, could apparently believe that divorce may not always be immoral; that illegitimate children do not bear any special and guaranteed form of curse; that there are ethical authorities outside of the Hebrew Bible; that men have drunk wine yet not died in the gutter; that the capitalistic system of distribution and the Baptist wedding-ceremony were not known in the Garden of Eden; that mushrooms are as edible as corn-beef hash; that the word

104

"dude" is no longer frequently used; that there are Ministers of the Gospel who accept evolution; that some persons of apparent intelligence and business ability do not always vote the Republican ticket straight; that it is not a universal custom to wear scratchy flannels next the skin in winter; that a violin is not inherently more immoral than a chapel organ; that some poets do not have long hair; and that Jews are not always peddlers or pants-makers. — Sinclair Lewis, *Main Street*

• And he absolutely had to find her at once to tell her that he adored her, but the large audience before him separated him from the door, and the notes reaching him through a succession of hands said that she was not available; that she was inaugurating a fire; that she had married an American businessman; that she had become a character in a novel; that she was dead. — Vladimir Nabokov, *Pale Fire*

• Oh, Starbuck! it is a mild, mild wind, and a mild looking sky. On such a day — very much such a sweetness as this — I struck my first whale — a boy-harpooneer of eighteen! Forty — forty — forty years ago! — ago! Forty years of continual whaling! forty years of privation, and peril, and storm-time! forty years on the pitiless sea! for forty years has Ahab forsaken the peaceful land, for forty years to make war on the horrors of the deep! Aye and yes, Starbuck, out of those forty years I have not spent three ashore. — Herman Melville, *Moby Dick*

• Fog everywhere. Fog up the river, where it flows among green aits and meadows; fog down the river, where it rolls defiled among the tiers of shipping and the waterside pollutions of a great (and dirty) city. Fog on the Essex marshes, fog on the Kentish heights. Fog creeping into the cabooses of collier-brigs; fog lying out on the yards and hovering in the rigging of great ships; fog drooping on the gunwales of barges and small boats. Fog in the eyes and throats of ancient Greenwich pensioners, wheezing by the firesides of their wards; fog in the stem and bowl of the afternoon pipe of the wrathful skipper, down in his close cabin; fog cruelly pinching the toes and fingers of his shivering little 'prentice boy on deck. — Charles Dickens, *Bleak House*

• Her antiquity in preceding and surviving succeeding tellurian generations: her nocturnal predominance: her satellitic dependence: her luminary reflection: her constancy under all her phases, rising and setting by her appointed times, waxing and waning: the forced invariability of her aspect: her indeterminate response to inaffirmative interrogation: her potency over effluent and refluent waters: her power to enamour, to mortify, to invest with beauty, to render insane, to incite to and aid delinquency: the tranquil inscrutability of her visage: the terribility of her isolated dominant resplendent propinquity: her omens of tempest and of calm: the stimulation of her light, her motion and her presence: the admonition of her craters, her arid seas, her silence: her splendour, when visible: her attraction, when invisible. — James Joyce, *Ulysses*

• They streamed aboard over three gangways, they streamed in urged by faith and the hope of paradise, they streamed in with a continuous tramp and shuffle of bare feet, without a word, a murmur, or a look back; and when clear of confining rails spread on all sides over the deck, flowed forward and aft, overflowed down the yawning hatchways, filled the inner recesses of the ship — like water filling a cistern, like water flowing into crevices and crannies, like water rising silently with the rim. — Joseph Conrad, *Lord Jim*

• Babbitt cranked with the unseen driver, with him waited through taut hours for the roar of the starting engine, with him agonized as the roar ceased and again began the infernal patient snap-ah-ah — a round, flat sound, a shivering, cold-morning sound, a sound infuriating and inescapable. — Sinclair Lewis, *Babbitt*

• There is a fear in their anticipation, for last time there had been many wounded, many tortured, many raped, many dead. — Margaret Drabble, *The Witch of Exmoor*

2.3.15 REPETITION: OF INITIAL CONSONANTS (ALLITERATION)

Where a person repeats the same consonant sounds at the beginning of successive words or syllables.

• The wine colors Candida's chicken portion pink. — Margaret Drabble, *The Seven Sisters*

• So we beat on, boats against the current, borne back ceaselessly into the past. — F. Scott Fitzgerald, *The*

Great Gatsby

• Sensible people get the greater part of their own dying done during their own lifetime. — Samuel Butler, *The Way of All Flesh*

• He resolved to be the first sampler of the first houri he would hire for his last house, and to live until then in laborious abstinence. — Vladimir Nabokov, *Ada, or Ardor*

• Beyond these tumuli habitations thickened, and the train came to a standstill in a tangle that was almost a town. — E. M. Forster, *Howard's End*

• Must I be foiled, fooled, fouled at every turn by wanton smashers and deliberate defilers. — Anthony Burgess, *The Eve of Saint Venus*

• The slack, soft insipid mansuetude of these females of the mind! — Lawrence Durrell, *Clea*

• Into the station it came blustering, with cloud and clangour. — Max Beerbohm, *Zuleika Dobson*

• I felt dull and flat and full of shattered visions. — Sylvia Plath, *The Bell Jar*

• They lived and laughed and loved and left. — James Joyce, *Finnegans Wake*

• And presently I was driving through the drizzle of the dying day, with the windshield wipers in full action but unable to cope with my tears. — Vladimir Nabokov, *Lolita*

• It filled the silence with an unnatural clamour, immense, mysterious, and menacing. — Edith Wharton, *Twilight Sleep*

• The men had stopped having careers and the women had stopped having babies. Liquor and love were left. — John Updike, *Couples*

• Noaks went, quickly. Echoes of his boots fell from the upper stairs and met the ascending susurrus of a silk skirt. — Max Beerbohm, *Zuleika Dobson*

• How can one sing the siren's song at sixty? — Margaret Drabble, *The Seven Sisters*

• He went up to bed well pleased, not only the master but the martyr of the household. — Sinclair Lewis, *Babbitt*

2.3.16 REPETITION: OF VOWEL SOUNDS IN ADJACENT WORDS (ASSONANCE)

Where a person repeats the same vowel sounds in successive words or syllables.

• English is a curiously expressive language. Womb, room, tomb. It sums up living in three words. — Anthony Burgess, *The End of the World News*

• I felt very still and very empty, the way the eye of a tornado must feel, moving dully along in the middle of the surrounding hullabaloo. — Sylvia Plath, *The Bell Jar*

• Indoors, in the Club, it's another world. It's all lightness and brightness and politeness. — Margaret Drabble, *The Seven Sisters*

• He was soon borne away by the waves, and lost in darkness and distance. — Mary Shelley, *Frankenstein*

• I call her a ghastly girl because she was a ghastly girl …. A droopy, soupy, sentimental exhibit, with melting eyes and a cooing voice and the most extraordinary views on such things as stars and rabbits. — P. G. Wodehouse, *The Code of the Woosters*

• Then as he began to move, in the sudden helpless orgasm, there awoke in her new strange thrills rippling inside her. Rippling,

rippling, rippling, like a flapping
overlapping of soft flames, soft as
feathers, running to points of
brilliance, exquisite, exquisite and
melting her all molten inside. — D.
H. Lawrence, *Lady Chatterley's
Lover*

• When they treacherously weaken
our efforts at soul-saving out here in
the field, and go in for a lot of
cussing and discussing and fussing
around with a lot of fool speculation
that don't do anybody any practical
good in the great work of bringing
poor sufferin' souls to peace, why
then I'm too busy to waste *my* time
on 'em, …. — Sinclair Lewis, *Elmer
Gantry*

2.3.17 REPETITION: OF A WORD IN A DIFFERENT FORM (POLYPTOTON)

*Where a person repeats the same
word used in different cases or
inflections.*

• There, in the world of the
mechanical greedy, greedy

114

mechanism and mechanized greed, sparkling with lights and gushing hot metal and roaring with traffic, there lay the vast evil thing, ready to destroy whatever did not conform.
— D. H. Lawrence, *Lady Chatterley's Lover*

• They think me mad — Starbuck does; but I am demoniac, I am madness maddened! — Herman Melville, *Moby Dick*

• For in tremendous extremities human souls are like drowning men; well enough they know they are in peril; well enough they know the causes of that peril; — nevertheless, the sea is the sea, and these drowning men do drown. — Herman Melville, *Pierre or The Ambiguities*

• Of all the cants which are canted in this canting world —though the cant of hypocrites may be the worst — the cant of criticism is the most tormenting! — Laurence Sterne, *Tristram Shandy*

• Our hero's unreasoning rage was fed by a not unreasonable jealousy. — Max Beerbohm, *Zuleika Dobson*

• With eager feeding food doth choke the feeder — William Shakespeare, *Richard II.*

• ... and the signora at every grimace and at every bow smiled a little smile and bowed a little bow. — Anthony Trollope, *Barchester Towers*

• He took up an oar and, since he was to have the credit of pulling, pulled. — Henry James, *The Ambassadors*

• By the time a partnership dissolves, it has dissolved. — John Updike, *Couples*

• It takes two people to make a murder: a murderer and a murderee. And a murderee is a man who is murderable. And a man who is murderable is a man who in a profound if hidden lust desires to be

murdered. — D. H. Lawrence,
Women in Love

• The Greeks are strong, and skillful
to their strength! Fierce to their
skill, and to their fierceness valiant.
— William Shakespeare, *Troilus and
Cressida*

2.3.18 REPETITION: OF THE FINAL WORDS OF A PHRASE, CLAUSE, OR SENTENCE AT THE BEGINNING OF THE NEXT PHRASE, CLAUSE, OR SENTENCE (ANADIPLOSIS)

*Where a person repeats a word or
phrase at the end of a phrase,
clause, or sentence at the beginning
of the following phrase, clause, or
sentence.*

• By the time they had swung in an
irregular way from prayer to psalm,
from psalm to history, from history
to poetry, and Mr. Bax was giving
out his text, she was in a state of
acute discomfort. — Virginia
Woolf, *The Voyage Out*

• If she stands up for him on account of the money, she will be a humbug. If she is a humbug, I shall see it. If I see it, I won't waste time with her. — Henry James, *Washington Square*

• Meanwhile, he with the slate continued moving slowly up and down, not without causing some stares to change into jeers, and some jeers into pushes, and some pushes, into punches.... — Herman Melville, T*he Confidence-Man: His Masquerade*

• My conscience hath a thousand several tongues, and every tongue brings in a several tale, and every tale condemns me for a villain. — William Shakespeare, *Richard III*

• The beach was a desert of heaps of sea and stones tumbling wildly about, and the sea did what it liked, and what it liked was destruction. — Charles Dickens, *A Tale of Two Cities*

• Now the quarry-discoverer is long before the stone-cutter; and the stone-cutter is long before the architect; and the architect is long before the temple; for the temple is the crown of the world. — Herman Melville, *Pierre or The Ambiguities*

• In the loveliest town of all, where the houses were white and high and the elms trees were green and higher than the houses, where the front yards were wide and pleasant and the back yards were bushy and worth finding out about, where the streets sloped down to the stream and the stream flowed quietly under the bridge, where the lawns ended in orchards and the orchards ended in fields and the fields ended in pastures and the pastures climbed the hill and disappeared over the top toward the wonderful wide sky, in this loveliest of all towns Stuart stopped to get a drink of sarsaparilla. — E. B. White, *Stuart Little*

2.3.19 REPETITION: OF WORDS IN THE OPPOSITE ORDER (CHIASMUS, EPANADOS, ANTIMETABOLE)

Where a person repeats a phrase in reverse order.

• I am Sam, Sam I am. — Dr. Seuss, *Green Eggs and Ham*

• Fool and coward! Coward and fool! — Herman Melville, *Pierre or The Ambiguities*

• Again the man rang and knocked, and knocked and rang again. — Charles Dickens, *Nicholas Nickleby*

• Fair is foul, and foul is fair. — William Shakespeare, *Macbeth*

• Nothing can cure the sole but the senses, just as nothing can cure the senses but the soul. — Oscar Wilde, *The Picture of Dorian Gray*

• Drat the file, and drat the bone! That is hard which should be soft, and that is soft which should be hard. — Herman Melville, *Moby Dick*

• I was there when needed. And now I am not needed and I am not there. — Margaret Drabble, *The Seven Sisters*

• I am a disappointed drudge, sir. I care for no man on earth, and no man on earth cares for me. — Charles Dickens, *A Tale of Two Cities*

• Our deeds determine us, as much as we determine our deeds. — George Eliot, *Adam Bede*

• I knew I had fallen in love with Lolita forever; but I also knew she would not be forever Lolita. — Vladimir Nabokov, *Lolita*

• Whenever I have gone there, there have been either so many people that I have not been able to see the pictures, which was dreadful, or so many pictures that I have not been able to see the people, which was

121

worse. — Oscar Wilde, *The Picture of Dorian Gray*

• For people who like that kind of thing, this is the kind of thing they like. — Max Beerbohm, *Zuleika Dobson*

• A most beastly place. Mudbank, mist, swamp, and work; work, swamp, mist, and mudbank — Charles Dickens, *Great Expectations*

• He neither thought a kick because he felt one nor felt a kick because he thought one. — Samuel Beckett, *Murphy*

2.3.20 REPETITION: OF AN IDEA IN DIFFERENT WORDS (CONGERIES, COMMORATIO)

Where a person repeats a point using different words.

•... which means to smash, to destroy, to annihilate all he had seen, known, loved, enjoyed or hated. — Joseph Conrad, *Lord Jim*

• I will not excuse you; you shall not be excused; excuses shall not be admitted; there is no excuse shall serve; you shall not be excused. — William Shakespeare, *Henry IV, Part 2*

• Alas! 'twill exasperate thy symptoms, — check thy perspirations, — evaporate thy spirits, — waste thy animal strength, dry up thy radical moisture, — bring thee into a costive habit of body, — impair thy health, — and hasten all the infirmities of thy old age. — Laurence Sterne, *Tristram Shandy*

• Heep has, on several occasions, to the best of my knowledge, information, and belief, systematically forged, to various entries, books, and documents, the signature of Mr. W. — Charles Dickens, *David Copperfield*

• But now I am cabin'd, cribb'd, confined, bound in to saucy doubts and fears. — William Shakespeare,

123

Macbeth

• Because he's a proud, haughty, consequential, turned-up-nosed peacock. — Charles Dickens, *Nicholas Nickleby*

• He was a bag of bones, a floppy doll, a broken stick, a maniac. — Jack Kerouac, *On the Road*

2.3.21 SUBSTITUTION: OF ONE GRAMMATICAL FORM FOR ANOTHER (ENALLAGE)

Where a person replaces one tense, number, person, or part of speech with another tense, number, person, or part of speech.

• And so if I am not emptied yet, I am is. — William Faulkner, *As I Lay Dying*

• Them's my sentiments. — William Makepeace Thackeray, *Vanity Fair*

• I takes my man Friday with me. — Daniel Defoe, *Robinson Crusoe*

• Is there not wars? Is there not employment? — William Shakespeare, *Henry IV, Part 2*

• My patience are exhausted. — James Joyce, *Ulysses*

2.3.22 SUBSTITUTION: OF ONE PART OF SPEECH FOR ANOTHER (ANTIMERIA)

Where a person replaces one part of speech with another part of speech.

• Heavens! Let me not suppose that she dares go about, Emma Woodhouse-ing me! — Jane Austen, *Emma*

• Bid them farewell, Cordelia, though unkind; thou losest here, a better where to find. — William Shakespeare, *King Lear*

• When the rain came to wet me once, and the wind to make me chatter, when the thunder would not peace at my bidding — there I found 'em, there I smelt 'em out. — William Shakespeare, *King Lear*

125

• Thank me no thankings, nor, proud me no prouds. — William Shakespeare, *Romeo and Juliet*

2.3.23 SUBSTITUTION: OF THE CORRECT SPELLING OF A WORD FOR A MISSPELLING OF IT (METAPLASMUS)

Where a person alters the spelling of a word by adding letters to it or subtracting letters from it or inverting letters in it.

• All Moanday, Tearday, Wailsday, Thumpsday, Frightday, Shatterday. — James Joyce, *Finnegans Wake*

• And even the like precurse of fierce events, as harbingers preceding still the fates and prologue to the omen coming on, have heaven and earth together demonstrated unto our climature and countrymen. — William Shakespeare, *Hamlet*

• "Day-ud cow," I said, expanding the word lusciously. "Day-ud cow, day-ud cow." — Alice Munro, *Lives of Girls and Women*

• What we know partakes in no small measure of the nature of what has so happily been called the unutterable or ineffable, so that any attempt to utter or eff it is doomed to fail, doomed, doomed to fail. — Samuel Beckett, *Watt*

2.3.24 SUBSTITUTION: OF THE CORRECT SPELLING OF A WORD FOR A MISSPELLING OF IT (TMESIS, INFIX)

Where a person inserts a word or words between the syllables of a word, between the parts of a compound word, or between the words in a phrase.

• This is not Romeo, he's some other where. — William Shakespeare, *Romeo and Juliet*

• It's a sort of long cocktail — he got the formula off a barman in Marrakesh or some-bloody-where. — Kingsley Amis, *Take a Girl Like You*

• *Ved'* ("it is, isn't it") sidesplitting to imagine that "Russia," instead of being a quaint synonym of Estoty, the American province extending from the Arctic no-longer-vicious Circle to the United States proper, was on Terra the name of a country, transferred as if by some sleight of land … — Vladimir Nabokov*, Ada, or Ardor*

• Miss voice of Kennedy answered, a second teacup poised, her gaze upon a page. — James Joyce, *Ulysses*

APPENDIX A

Though not a rhetorical figure, the inclusion or omission of punctuation marks is a device that some authors use to achieve a particular effect or convey a particular impression.

A.1 INCLUSION OF PUNCTUATION

Where a person uses punctuation marks when we normally might not expect them.

• And I too am at an end, when I am there, my eyes close, my sufferings cease and I end, I wither as the living can not. And if I went on listening to that far whisper, silent long since and which I still hear, I would learn still more, about this. But I will listen no longer, for the time being, to that far whisper, for I do not like it, I fear it. But it is not a sound like the other sounds, that you listen to, when you choose, and can sometimes silence, by going away or stopping your ears, no, but it is a sound which begins to rustle in your head, without your knowing how, or why. — Samuel Beckett, *Molloy*

A.2 OMISSION OF PUNCTUATION

Where a person does not use punctuation marks when we normally might expect them.

• She was looking at me in the cool north indigo duskiness of the room with such a humble pleading diffident rueful tender look upon her face, and her drooping hands were opened to me in a sort of Oriental gesture of abandonment and homage. — Iris Murdoch, *The Black Prince*

• ... one minute she was standing there the next he was yelling and pulling at her dress they went into the hall and up the stairs yelling and shoving at her up the stairs to the bathroom door and stopped her back against the door and her arm across her face yelling and trying to shove her into the bathroom when she came in to supper T. P. was feeding him he started again just whimpering at first until she touched him then he yelled she stood there her eyes like cornered rats then I was running in the gray darkness it smelled of rain and all flower scents the damp warm air released and crickets sawing away in the grass ... — William Faulkner, *The Sound and the Fury*

• ... stifling it was today Im glad I burned the half of those old Freemans and Photo Bits leaving things like that lying about hes getting very careless and threw the rest of them up in the W C Ill get him to cut them tomorrow for me instead of having them there for the next year to get a few pence for them have him asking wheres last Januarys paper and all those old overcoats. ... — James Joyce, *Ulysses*

Appendix B

More Elegant Paragraphs

Read these further examples of elegant English at your leisure, and from each you might glean some clarity of expression, some recognition of emotion, some novelty of thought, some device of rhetoric that, in more contemporary writing, you seldom will notice. From these paragraphs also you might learn that language can be written elegantly, with care and cleverness.

1. I remember the morning when our butcher's boy brought the news that the first German flag had been hung out on the balcony of the Ministry of War. Now I thought, the Latin will boil over! And I wanted to be there to see. I hurried down the quiet rue de Martignac, turned the corner of the Place Sainte Clotilde, and came on an orderly crowd filling the street before the Ministry of War.

The crowd was so orderly that the few pacific gestures of the police easily cleared a way for passing cabs, and for the military motors perpetually dashing up. It was composed of all classes, and there were many family groups, with little boys straddling their mothers' shoulders, or lifted up by the policemen when they were too heavy for their mothers. It is safe to say that there was hardly a man or woman of that crowd who had not a soldier at the front; and there before them hung the enemy's first flag — a splendid silk flag, white and black and crimson, and embroidered in gold. It was the flag of an Alsatian regiment — a regiment of Prussianized Alsace. It symbolized all they most abhorred in the whole abhorrent job that lay ahead of them; it symbolized also their finest ardour and their noblest hate, and the reason why, if every other reason failed, France could never lay down arms till the last of such flags was low. — Edith Wharton, *Fighting France*

133

2. We shall not flag or fail. We shall go on to the end. We shall fight in France, we shall fight on the seas and oceans, we shall fight with growing confidence and growing strength in the air, we shall defend our island, whatever the cost may be. We shall fight on the beaches, we shall fight on the landing grounds, we shall fight in the fields and in the streets, we shall fight in the hills; we shall never surrender. — Winston Churchill, Speech

3. The moon rises ruddy from that solemn obscurity of jebel like a mighty beacon: — and the morrow will be as this day, days deadly drowned in the sun of the summer wilderness. — Charles M. Doughty, *Travels in Arabia Deserta*

4. Sleep is most graceful in an infant; soundest, in one who has been tired in the open air; completest, to the seaman after a hard voyage; most welcome, to the mind haunted with one idea; most touching to look at, in the parent that has wept; lightest, in the playful child; proudest, in the bride adored. — Leigh Hunt, *A Few Thoughts on Sleep*

5. Let me wither and wear out mine age in a discomfortable, in an unwholesome, in a penurious prison, and so pay my debts with my bones, and recompense the wastefulness of my youth, with the beggary of mine age; let me wither in a spittle under sharp, and foul, and infamous diseases, and so recompense the wantonness of my youth, with that loathsomeness in mine age. — John Donne, *Let Me Wither*

6. Somewhere, I knew not where — somehow, I knew not how — by some beings, I knew not whom — a battle, a strife, an agony, was conducting, — was evolving like a great drama, or piece of music; with which my sympathy was the more insupportable from my confusion as to its place, its cause, its nature, and its possible issue. I, as is usual in dreams (where, of necessity, we make ourselves central to every movement), had the power, and yet had not the power, to decide it. I had the power, if I could raise myself, to will it; and yet again had not the power, for the weight of twenty Atlantics was upon me, or the oppression of inexpiable guilt. "Deeper than ever plummet sounded," I lay inactive. Then, like a chorus, the passion deepened. Some greater interest was at stake; some mightier cause than ever yet the sword had pleaded, or trumpet had proclaimed. Then came sudden alarms; hurryings to and fro; trepidations of innumerable fugitives. I knew not whether from the good cause or the bad; darkness and lights; tempest and human faces; and at last, with the sense that all was lost, female forms, and the features that were worth all the world to me, and but a moment allowed, — and clasped hands, and heart-breaking partings, and then — everlasting farewells! and, with a sigh, such as the caves of hell

136

sighed when the incestuous mother uttered the abhorred name of death, the sound was reverberated — everlasting farewells! and again, and yet again reverberated — everlasting farewells! — Thomas de Quincey, *Confessions of an Opium Eater*

7. If then the power of speech is as great as any that can be named, — if the origin of language is by many philosophers considered nothing short of divine — if by means of words the secrets of the heart are brought to light, pain of soul is relieved, hidden grief is carried off, sympathy conveyed, experience recorded, and wisdom perpetuated, — if by great authors the many are drawn up into unity, national character is fixed, a people speaks, the past and the future, the East and the West are brought into communication with each other, — if such men are, in a word, the spokesmen and the prophets of the human family — it will not answer to make light of Literature or to neglect its study: rather we may be

137

sure that, in proportion as we master it in whatever language, and imbibe its spirit, we shall ourselves become in our own measure the ministers of like benefits to others — be they many or few, be they in the obscurer or the more distinguished walks of life — who are united to us by social ties, and are within the sphere of our personal influence. — John Henry Newman, *The Idea of a University*

8. Great is all townsmen's dread of the Beduw, as if they were the demons of this wild waste earth, ever ready to assail the Haj passengers; and there is no Beduwy durst chop logic in the dark with these often ferocious shooters, that might answer him with lead and who are heard, from time to time, firing backward into the desert all night.... — Charles M. Doughty, *Travels in Arabia Deserta*

9. The character of the Italian statesman seems, at first sight, a collection of contradictions, a phantom as monstrous as the portress of hell in Milton, half divinity, half snake, majestic and beautiful above, grovelling and poisonous below. We see a man whose thoughts and words have no connection with each other, who never hesitates at an oath when he wishes to seduce, who never wants a pretext when he is inclined to betray. His cruelties spring, not from the heat of blood, or the insanity of uncontrolled power, but from deep and cool meditation. His passions, like well-trained troops, are impetuous by rule, and in their most headstrong fury never forget the discipline to which they have been accustomed. His whole soul is occupied with vast and complicated schemes of ambition, yet his aspect and language exhibit nothing but philosophical moderation. Hatred and revenge eat into his heart; yet every look is a cordial smile, every gesture a familiar caress. He never excites the suspicion of his adversaries by petty provocations. His purpose is disclosed, only when it is accomplished. His face is unruffled, his speech is courteous, till vigilance is laid asleep, till a vital point is exposed, till a sure aim is taken; and then he strikes for the first and last time. Military courage, the boast of the sottish German, of the frivolous and prating Frenchman, of the romantic and arrogant Spaniard, he neither possesses nor values. He shuns danger, not because he is insensible to shame, but because, in the society in which he lives, timidity has ceased to be shameful. To do an injury openly is, in his estimation, as wicked as to do it secretly, and far less profitable. With him the most honorable means are those which are the surest, the speediest, and the darkest. He cannot comprehend how a man should scruple to deceive those whom he does not scruple to destroy. He would think it madness to declare open hostilities against rivals whom he might stab in a friendly embrace, or poison in a consecrated wafer. —

Thomas Babington Macaulay,
Machiavelli

10. The beautiful metropolis of
America is by no means so clean a
city as Boston, but many of its
streets have the same
characteristics; except that the
houses are not quite so fresh-
coloured, the sign-boards are not
quite so gaudy, the gilded letters not
quite so golden, the bricks not quite
so red, the stone not quite so white,
the blinds and area railings not
quite so green, the knobs and plates
upon the street-doors not quite so
bright and twinkling. — Charles
Dickens, *American Notes*

11. These instances (and many
more might be collected) are
sufficient to afford us some insight
into the analogy of nature, and to
show us, that the pleasure, which
poets, orators, and musicians give
us, by exciting grief, sorrow,
indignation, compassion, is not so
extraordinary or paradoxical, as it
may at first sight appear. The force
141

of imagination, the energy of expression, the power of numbers, the charms of imitation; all these are naturally, of themselves, delightful to the mind: And when the object presented lays also hold of some affection, the pleasure still rises upon us, by the conversion of this subordinate movement into that which is predominant. The passion, though, perhaps, naturally, and when excited by the simple appearance of a real object, it may be painful; yet is so smoothed, and softened, and mollified, when raised by the finer arts, that it affords the highest entertainment. — David Hume, *Of Tragedy*

12. In art, in taste, in life, in speech, you decide from feeling, and not from reason; that is, from the impression of a number of things on the mind, which impression is true and well founded, though you may not be able to analyze or account for it in the several particulars. In a gesture you use, in a look you see, in a tone you hear, you judge of the

142

expression, propriety, and meaning
from habit, not from reason or rules;
that is to say, from innumerable
instances of like gestures, looks,
and tones, in innumerable other
circumstances, variously modified,
which are too many and too refined
to be all distinctly recollected, but
which do not therefore operate the
less powerfully upon the mind and
eye of taste. Shall we say that these
impressions (the immediate stamp
of nature) do not operate in a given
manner till they are classified and
reduced to rules, or is not the rule
itself grounded, upon the truth and
certainty of that natural operation?
How then can the distinction of the
understanding as to the manner on
which they operated be necessary to
their producing their due and
uniform effect upon the mind? If
certain effects did not regularly arise
out of certain causes in mind as well
as matter, there could be no rule
given for them: nature does not
follow the rule, but suggests it.
Reason is the interpreter and critic
of nature and genius, not their law-

giver and judge. — William Hazlitt, *On Genius and Common Sense*

13. I do here in the name of all the learned and polite persons of the nation, complain to your Lordship, as First Minister, that our language is extremely imperfect; that its daily improvements are by no means in proportion to its daily corruptions; and the pretenders to polish and refine it, have chiefly multiplied abuses and absurdities; and, that in many instances, it offends against every part of grammar. ... Whether our language or the French will decline as fast as the Roman did, is a question that would perhaps admit more debate than it is worth. There were many reasons for the corruptions of the last: As, the change of their government into a tyranny, which ruined the study of eloquence, there being no further use of encouragement for popular orators. — Jonathan Swift, *Proposal for Correcting, Improving and Ascertaining the English Tongue*

14. That Government is at once dreaded and contemned; that the laws are despoiled of all their respected and salutary terrors; that their inaction is a subject of ridicule, and their exertion of abhorrence; that rank, and office, and title, and all the solemn plausibilities of the world, have lost their reverence and effect; that our foreign politics are as much deranged as our domestic economy; that our dependencies are slackened in their affection, and loosened from their obedience; that we know neither how to yield nor how to enforce; that hardly anything above or below, abroad or at home, is sound and entire; but that disconnection and confusion, in offices, in parties, in families, in Parliament, in the nation, prevail beyond the disorders of any former time: these are facts universally admitted and lamented. — Edmund Burke, *Thoughts on the Present Discontents*

15. Now and then, in the course of the century, a great man of science, like Darwin; a great poet, like Keats; a fine critical spirit, like M. Renan; a supreme artist, like Flaubert, has been able to isolate himself, to keep himself out of reach of the clamorous claims of others, to stand 'under the shelter of the wall,' as Plato puts it, and so to realise the perfection of what was in him, to his own incomparable gain, and to the incomparable and lasting gain of the whole world. These, however, are exceptions. The majority of people spoil their lives by an unhealthy and exaggerated altruism — are forced, indeed, so to spoil them. They find themselves surrounded by hideous poverty, by hideous ugliness, by hideous starvation. — Oscar Wilde, *The Soul of Man Under Socialism*

16. But it is we who are the morbid exceptions; it is we who are the criminal class. This should be our great comfort. The vast mass of humanity, with their vast mass of idle books and idle words, have never doubted and never will doubt that courage is splendid, that

146

fidelity is noble, that distressed ladies should be rescued, and vanquished enemies spared. There are a large number of cultivated persons who doubt these maxims of daily life, just as there are a large number of persons who believe they are the Prince of Wales; and I am told that both classes of people are entertaining conversationalists. But the average man or boy writes daily in these great gaudy diaries of his soul, which we call Penny Dreadfuls, a plainer and better gospel than any of those iridescent ethical paradoxes that the fashionable change as often as their bonnets. — G. K. Chesterton, *A Defence of Penny Dreadfuls*

17. Among this congregation, were some evil-looking young women, and beetle-browed young men; but not many — perhaps that kind of characters kept away. Generally, the faces (those of the children excepted) were depressed and subdued, and wanted colour. Aged people were there, in every variety.

Mumbling, blear-eyed, spectacled, stupid, deaf, lame; vacantly winking in the gleams of sun that now and then crept in through the open doors, from the paved yard; shading their listening ears, or blinking eyes, with their withered hands; poring over their books, leering at nothing, going to sleep, crouching and drooping in corners. There were weird old women, all skeleton within, all bonnet and cloak without, continually wiping their eyes with dirty dusters of pocket-handkerchiefs; and there were ugly old crones, both male and female, with a ghastly kind of contentment upon them which was not at all comforting to see. Upon the whole, it was the dragon, Pauperism, in a very weak and impotent condition; toothless, fangless, drawing his breath heavily enough, and hardly worth chaining up. — Charles Dickens, *A Walk in a Workhouse*

18. Whatsoever therefore is consequent to a time of War, where every man is Enemy to everyman, the same consequent to the time wherein men live without other security than what their own strength and their own invention shall furnish them withal. In such condition there is no place for Industry, because the fruit thereof is uncertain: and consequently no Culture of the Earth; no Navigation, nor use of the commodities that may be imported by Sea; no commodious Building; no Instruments of moving and removing such things as require much force; no Knowledge of the face of the Earth; no account of Time; no Arts; no Letters; no Society; and which is worst of all, continual fear, and danger of violent death; and the life of man, solitary, poor, nasty, brutish, and short. — Thomas Hobbes, *Leviathan*

APPENDIX C

SILENCE, LANGUAGE, AND SOCIETY

1. Being silent is the chance to think, to talk to oneself, and it is preferable to much of what we say aloud. We need to speak, as we need to write, with more deliberation and clarity. Our sanity and our society depend on it. Thought is borne of quiet, of internal talk. In today's money-grubbing, entertainment-ridden, fear-induced society, there is scant value in being still and thinking for oneself.

2. Without the temperament to listen to our own thoughts and feelings, without the resolve to be silent and still, we will never make much of an impression on others. We will think as others think, speak as others speak, act as others act, but these, alone, are poor talents, barren of any true ability.

3. Do not live your life only to mimic what others say and do; live your life to learn and be true to who you are. Fail to feel, fear to think, and you'll manage no more than everyone else who avoided stillness and shunned silence.

4. Let us have time to be silent and still, time to reflect on the past, ponder the present, and think about the future; without it, no one is knowable.

5. Be silent and all you neglected to consider, all you failed to feel, all you hoped to say will unfold before you.

6. About silence little can be said. Silence soon succumbs to speech.

7. Even today — subjected as we are to the apotheosis of popular culture — using the English language respectfully helps us maintain a sense of ourselves and our values. To do otherwise, to disregard the ways of our words, is to forsake our humanity and, perhaps, even forfeit our future.

8. Inadequate though they may be, words distinguish us from all other living things. Only we humans can reflect on the past and plan for the future; it is language that allows us to do so. Indeed, our worth is partly in our words. Effective use of language — clear writing and speaking — is a measure of our humanness.

9. The point of learning new words is not to impress your friends or to seem more intelligent than they. The point is to see more, to understand more. An ever-increasing vocabulary uncovers connections, introduces spheres, and — in reminding us that there are words for all thoughts, all feelings, all behaviors, all things — upholds all humankind.

10. The less well we use the language, the less thoughtful, cogent, and communicative we likely are.

11. When they do their work best, words help people communicate; they promote understanding between people. And this, being well understood, is precisely the goal we should all aspire to when writing and speaking. As obvious as this seems, it is not a goal we commonly achieve.

12. Words often ill serve their purpose. When they do their work badly, words militate against us. Poor grammar, sloppy syntax, abused words, misspelled words, and other infelicities of style impede communication and advance only misunderstanding.

13. We often believe that many words are better than few. Perhaps we imagine that the more we say, the more we know or the more others will think we know, or that the more obscure our writing is, the more profound our thoughts are.
153

Seldom, of course, is this so. A superfluity of words conceals more than it reveals.

14. As never before, people do as others do, speak as others speak, and think as others think. The cliché is king. Nothing is so reviled as individuality. We imitate one another lest we be left alone. We want to fit in, to be part of the crowd. We want groups to engulf us and institutions to direct us.

15. Nothing turns a sentence so quickly as a cliché. The more of these sentences we read, the more our disposition sours and our disgust mounts.

16. Many of us seek to enhance our self-importance by using ostentatious language. We may believe that the more words we use, or the more elaborate our language, the more intelligent we sound and important we are. We may recognize the thinness of our thoughts and try to give them added weight by using polysyllabic words. Or we may chatter endlessly as though each word were further proof of our presence.

17. Some people through expedient, euphemistic, or circumlocutory language, strive to conceal their actions, to becloud what they say and do. With words they do whatever they please and, in so doing, manage to confuse our perception of their deeds and, even, their identity.

18. Academics and social scientists regularly try to give more prestige to their disciplines, and themselves, by breeding their own vocabularies.

19. Whereas a witticism is a clever remark or phrase — indeed, the height of expression — a dimwitticism is the converse; it is a commonplace remark or phrase. Dimwitticisms are worn-out words and phrases; they are expressions that dull our reason and dim our insight, formulas that we rely on

155

when we are too lazy to express what we think or even to discover how we feel. The more we use them the more we conform — in thought and feeling — to everyone else who uses them.

20. Dimwitticisms are categorized by the following thirteen types:

<u>Grammatical gimmicks</u>: Quite simply, *and everything* is a babbler's way of describing what he was unable to. This phrase and so many others like it — *and everything like that; and stuff (things); and (or) stuff (things) like that; and this and that; anyway; I mean; (and that) kind of stuff (thing); or something or other; or whatever; this, that, and the other (thing); you had to be there* — are grammatical gimmicks that we use to make up for the misfashioned words that precede them.

These are devices that we resort to whenever we are unable to explain adequately our thoughts or feelings. Grammatical gimmicks attest to just how dull and dimwitted we have become.

Ineffectual phrases: Ineffectual phrases are the expressions people use to delay or obstruct, to bewilder or make weary. The intent of those who use ineffectual phrases is to make it appear as though their sentences are more substantial than they actually are, but not one sentence is made more meaningful by their inclusion: *(please) be advised that; I'll tell you (something); it has come to (my) attention; it is important to realize (that); it is interesting to note (that); make no mistake (about it); (to) take this opportunity (to); the fact of the matter is; the fact remains; the thing about it is; what happened (is).*

How a person speaks often reveals how he thinks. And how he thinks determines how he behaves. A person who speaks ineffectually may think ineffectually, and a person who thinks ineffectually may

behave ineffectually — perhaps
badly.

Ineffectual phrases add only to our
being ineffectual people.

<u>Inescapable pairs</u>: In an inescapable
pair, the first word means much the
same as the second or so often
accompanies the second that any
distinction between them is, in
effect, forfeited.

Only occasionally, that is, do we see
the word *allied* without the word
closely; asset without *valuable; baby*
without *beautiful; balance* without
delicate; distinction without *dubious;
error* without *egregious; tied* without
inextricably; missed without *sorely;
poverty* without *abject; principle*
without *basic.*

And more often than not we find the
word *aid* joined to *abet; alive* joined
to *well; effective* joined to *efficient;
hope* joined to *pray; hue* joined to
cry; pure joined to *simple.*

When two words are treated as though they were one — the plight of every inescapable pair — our keenness is compromised, our discernment endangered.

No longer does every word tell; the words themselves have become witless.

<u>Infantile phrases</u>: Any thought or feeling in which these expressions are found is likely to be made instantly laughable: *absolutely, positively; all of the above; because (that's why); because why?; (as) compared to what?; going on (19); I'll bet you any amount of money; in no way, shape, or form; intestinal fortitude; it takes one to know one; me, myself, and I; mission accomplished; mutual admiration society; never (not) in a million years; real, live; really and truly; (you) started it; (I) take it back; the feeling's mutual; the (L)-word; (my) whole, entire life; with a capital (A); (62) years young; (a) zillion(s) (of).*

Also included among these phrases that strike all but the dimwitted as derisory are notorious advertising slogans (*inquiring minds want to know; where's the beef*), song and film titles (*a funny thing happened to me on the way to; I can't get no satisfaction*), and alliterative or rhymed phrases (*a bevy of beauties; chrome dome*).

Other infantile phrases are more disturbing, for they reveal an adolescent, unformed reasoning. Explanations like *in the wrong place at the wrong time, it just happened, it's a free country, and everything's (it's all) relative* are as farcical as they are possibly fallacious.

Moribund metaphors: Metaphors, like similes, should have the briefest of lives. Their vitality depends on their evanescence.

Yet must we ever endure the dimwitted *(it's) a jungle (out there), an emotional roller coaster, a stroll (walk) in the park, (like) being run*

*over (getting hit) by a (Mack) truck,
(as) cool as a cucumber, everything
but the kitchen sink, (as) hungry as a
horse, leak like a sieve, light at the
end of the tunnel, out to lunch, over
the hill, pass like ships in the night,
(as) phony as a three-dollar bill, (a)
piece of cake, rule the roost, window
of opportunity, (every parent's) worst
nightmare,* and countless other
metaphors that characterize people
as dull, everyday speakers and
writers, indeed, as platitudinarians?
Nothing new do they tell us. Nothing
more do they show us.

Moreover, if it weren't for our
plethora of metaphors, especially,
sports images — *above par, a new
ballgame, batting a thousand, do
(make) an end run around, down for
the count, hit a home run, off base,
pull no punches, stand on the
sidelines, step up to the plate, took
the ball and ran with it* — and war
images — *a call to arms, an uphill
battle, battle lines are drawn, draw
fire, earn his stripes, first line of
defense, in the trenches, on the firing*

line, take by storm — men and, even, women would be far less able to articulate their thoughts. We would speak and write more haltingly than we already do; our thoughts and feelings more misshapen than they already are.

We rely on moribund metaphors not because we feel they make our speech and writing more vivid and inviting but because we fail to learn how to express ourselves otherwise; we know not the words.

In truth, the more of these metaphors we use, the less effective is our speech and writing. Neither interesting nor persuasive, their expression fatigues us where we thought it would inform us, annoys us where we believed it would amuse us, and benumbs us where we hoped it would inspire us.

<u>Overworked words</u>: The broader your knowledge of words, the greater your ability to express yourself precisely and persuasively.

Many speakers and writers, however, depend on certain words — overworked words like *action, actively, amazing, appreciate, approach, attitude, awesome, basically, crisis, definitely, devastate, effect, excellence, great, impact, implement, incredible, interesting, lasting, major, meaningful, mind — set, natural, nice, ongoing, parameter, pretty, really, scenario, significant, situation, strange, thing, unbelievable, very, weird.*

Words, when overworked, diminish the meaning of all that they are used to describe. Our remarks and questions both are enfeebled by these tired terms. Nothing that we express with these overworked words has the force or effectiveness of less habitually spoken, less repeatedly written words. Moreover, since a person understands little more than what the words he is knowledgeable of convey — a word means only so much — to rely on so few words reveals just how limited a person's understanding of himself, and those about him, is.

Our knowledge of the world increases as our familiarity with words does.

<u>Plebeian sentiments</u>: Plebeian sentiments reflect the views and values of the least thoughtful among us: *be nice; (I) gave (him) the best years of (my) life; (it) gives (me) something to do; (these things) happen to other people, not to (me); I (just) don't think about it; I just work here; I'm bored (he's boring); (it) keeps (me) busy; (it's) something to look forward to; there are no words to describe (express); you think too much; what can you do; why me?*

What's more, these expressions, base as they are, blunt our understanding and quash our creativity. They actually shield us from our thoughts and feelings, from any profound sense of ourselves.

People who use these expressions have not become who they were meant to be.

<u>Popular prescriptions</u>: Powerless to repeat an author's epigram, unfit to recite a poet's verse, more than many of us are utterly able to echo a society's slogans and clichés: *absence makes the heart grow fonder; actions speak louder than words; a picture is worth a thousand words; beauty is in the eye of the beholder; better late than never; do as I say, not as I do; forgive and forget; hope for the best but expect the worst; it takes two; keep (your) nose to the grindstone; live and learn; misery loves company; money isn't everything; neither a borrower nor a lender be; take it one day (step) at a time; the best things in life are free; the meek shall inherit the earth; the sooner the better; time flies when you're having fun; two wrongs don't make a right; what goes around, comes around; you can't be all things to all people; you can't have everything.*

165

Popular prescriptions are the platitudes and proverbs by which people live their lives. It is these dicta that determine who we are and how we act; they define our intellectual and moral makeup.

Dull-witted speakers and writers depend on prescriptions like these to guide them through life. For this poor populace, life is, we may surmise, laid out. From the popular or proper course, there is scant deviation.

Popular prescriptions endure not for their sincerity but for their simplicity. We embrace them because they make all they profess to explain and all they profess to prescribe seem plain and uncomplicated.

Inexorably, we become as simple as they — we people, we platitudes.

Quack equations: *a deal is a deal; a politician is a politician; a promise is a promise; a rule is a rule; enough is enough; ethics is ethics; fair is fair; God is love; it is what it is; less is more; more is better; perception is reality; (what's) right is right; seeing is believing; talk is cheap; the law is the law is the law; what happened happened; what's done is done.* This is the sort of simplicity much favored by mountebanks and pretenders, by businesspeople and politicians. Quack equations too readily explain behavior that the undiscerning may otherwise find inexplicable and justify attitudes that they may otherwise find unjustifiable. No remedies for shoddy reasoning, no restoratives for suspect thinking, these palliatives soothe only our simple-mindedness.

Equally distressing is that there is no end to these quack equations: *alcohol is alcohol; he is who he is; math is math; money is money is money; people are people; plastic is plastic; prejudice is prejudice; their reasoning is their reasoning; the past is the past; wrong is wrong.* Forever being fabricated and continually being merchandized, shoddy thinking is far more easily dispensed than sound thinking.

<u>Suspect superlatives</u>: In dimwitted usage, superlatives are suspect. That which seems most laudable is often least, that which seems topmost, bottommost, that which seems best, worst: *an amazing person; (I'm) a perfectionist; area of expertise; celebrity; class; gentleman; great; personal friend; pursuit of excellence; the best and (the) brightest; the rich and famous.*

<u>Torpid terms</u>: Torpid terms are vapid words and phrases that we use in place of vital ones: *a majority of; a moving experience; a number of; a step (forward) in the right direction; cautiously optimistic; (take) corrective action; degree; effectuate; extent; (a) factor; incumbent upon; indicate; input; leaves a little (a lot; much; something) to be desired; move forward; negative feelings; off-putting; operative; prioritize;*

*proactive; pursuant to; remedy the
situation; represent(s); (the) same;
send a message; shocked (surprised)
and saddened (dismayed).* Formulas
as flat as these keep us dumb and
dispassionate. They elicit the least
from us.

With these unsound formulas, little
can be communicated and still less
can be accomplished. Torpid terms
interfere with our understanding
and with our taking action; they
thwart our thinking and frustrate
our feeling.

<u>Withered words</u>: There are many
rare and wonderful words that we
would do well to become familiar
with — words that would revitalize
us for our revitalizing them — words
like *bedizen; bootless; caliginous;
compleat; cotquean; hebdomadal;
helpmeet; logorrhea; quondam; wont.*

Withered words, however — words
like *albeit; amidst; amongst;
behoove; betwixt; forsooth;
perchance; said; save; thence;*
169

unbeknownst; verily; whence; wherein; whereon; wherewith; whilst —are archaic and deserve only to be forgotten.

People who use them say little that is memorable.

<u>Wretched redundancies</u>: Reckless writers and slipshod speakers use many words where few would do: *advance planning; at this time; consensus of opinion; dead body; due to the fact that; first and foremost; free gift; just recently; in advance of; in and of itself; in spite of the fact that; in terms of; make a determination; on a ... basis; on the part of; past experience; period of time; (the) reason (why) is because; refer back; the single best (most); until such time as.* Yet for all the words, their expression is but impoverished; more words do not necessarily signify more meaning.

Life is measured by its meaning, and a good deal of that meaning is inherent in the words we use. If so many of our words are superfluous

— and thus do not signify — so much of our life is, ineluctably, meaningless.

In the end, we are no more superfluous than are the words we use.

21. Each dimwitticism is a failure to write clearly and compellingly, an admission that the writer or speaker could not manage an original thought or a better turn of phrase, or could not be bothered to think of one. Dimwitticisms yield only facile writing, only false sentiment.

22. Within sentences, among thoughts struggling to be expressed and ideas seeking to be understood, dimwitticisms ravage the writer's efforts as much as they do the reader's, the speaker's as much as the listener's.

23. People who rely on dimwitticisms appear to express themselves more fluently and articulately than those few who do not. But this is a sham articulateness, for without the use of phrases like *left holding the bag, left out in the cold, her worst nightmare, and that type of stuff, basically, level the playing field, stick out like a sore thumb, arrive on the scene, shocked and saddened, it is interesting to note, in the wrong place at the wrong time, with a capital M, a breath of fresh air, incredible,* and *definitely,* most people would stammer helplessly.

24. One of the difficulties with dimwitticisms is that, because they are so familiar, people will most often use them thoughtlessly. Manacled as people are to these well-worn phrases, original thoughts and fresh words are often unreachable.

25. Those of us who speak well are thought false and formal; the more articulate you are, the less approachable you are thought to be. It is not what you say that revolts others, but the structure, modest or monumental though it may be, of your sentences, the style, not the substance, of your speech.

26. The irony of this is as painful as it is patent. Speech, a predominantly, perhaps uniquely, human device, which is designed, as no other human means is, to help people communicate, to promote understanding between people, serves, when polished and precise, to make the speaker appear inaccessible.

27. It is scarcely those who speak badly who hamper our language's capacity to communicate, it is we who speak well, who delight in style and subtleties of syntax rather than in jargon and gibberish. As odious as this is, more odious still is that it signifies the exaltation of shoddiness. Soundness and sense have had their day; shoddiness now has the dais.

28. A person who expresses himself with genuineness instead of in
173

jargon, with feeling instead of in formulas, is capable as few have been, as few are, and as few will be; this is a person to heed.

29. All it takes for a solecism to become standard English is people misusing or misspelling the word. And if enough people do so, lexicographers will enter the originally misused or misspelled word into their dictionaries, and descriptive linguists will embrace it as a further example of the evolution of English.

30. Dictionaries are ever more a catalogue of confusions, a list of illiteracies. Dictionaries acknowledge the errors that people make; by acknowledging them they, in effect, endorse them; by endorsing them, they are thought correct by the dull, duped public. Ultimately, all words will mean whatever we think they mean, indeed, whatever we want them to mean.

31. That a president can ask *Is our children learning?* a basketball star can use the word *conversate,* a well-known college professor can say *vociferous* when he means *voracious,* and another can scold a student for using the word *juggernaut* because she believes it means *jigaboo* is disturbing. But these are precisely the sorts of errors, if enough people make them, that lexicographers will one day include in their dictionaries.

32. Consider these popular usages: the childish *way* (and, even, *way way*) instead of, for example, *far* (The Internet is potentially *way* more powerful than television ever dreamed of being.); the illiterate *like* instead of *as* (She voted based on the information given to her at the time — just *like* President Bush did, just *like* Senator Edwards did, just *like* all senators did at that time.); the grotesque *would have* instead of *had* (If she *would have* done her homework, she would know that.); the foolish *friend* instead of *befriend* (Talk to your high school-aged teens

175

about whether or not they're comfortable letting you *friend* them.). There is scant accuracy, clarity, or elegance in these usages that the lexicographers and linguists, the, let us call them, *lexlings* applaud and promote.

33. Over the last forty and more years, linguists and lexicographers have conspired to transform an indispensable reference work into an increasingly useless, increasingly dangerous one. Lexicographers are no longer harmless.

34. Lexlings help ensure that we — or those people who still, for what reasons we can only wonder, pay any attention to the dictionary — speak and write like every other ignoramus.

35. Dictionaries, today, do not necessarily tell us the correct meanings of words; they simply tell us how people use words — hardly a good measure of meaning.

36. The meanings of some words do change over time, but much language change is due to ignorance, confusion, and imitation, among the qualities that define humanity best. Lexicography and linguistics may be the only professions that accept ignorance so readily and reward it so unabashedly.

37. Other words are coined and created in an attempt to define something for which perhaps there has not been sufficient understanding or something that is newly discovered or recognized. "Lexlings" is a useful contribution: it means both *lex*icographers and *ling*uists, and expresses an opinion of both with the diminutive suffix -*ling*.

38. Nothing dissuades a person quite so quickly from reading your writing as your having misused a word. Know the meanings of the words you use. Meaning, despite the meaninglessness, the idiocy, that engulfs us all, still matters.

39. The only meaning in life is what we assign to it. Similarly, we assign meaning to the principal way we express meaning, to our words. If we fail to observe the meanings of our words, we contribute to the meaninglessness of our lives.

40. Where meanings are mangled, minds are also.

41. Lexicographers are descriptivists, language liberals. The use of *disinterested* to mean *uninterested* does not displease a descriptivist. A prescriptivist, by contrast, is a language conservative, a person interested in maintaining standards and correctness in language use. To prescriptivists, *disinterested* in the sense of *uninterested* is the mark of uneducated people who do not know the distinction between the two words. And if there are enough uneducated people saying

disinterested when they mean
uninterested or *indifferent*,
lexicographers enter the definition
into their dictionaries. Indeed, the
distinction between these words has
all but vanished owing largely to
irresponsible writers and boneless
lexicographers.

42. If we ignore the distinctions
between words, we begin to ignore
or disapprove of the distinctions
between people; individuality,
which, even now, is not favorably
regarded, will become increasingly
frowned upon, eventually unlawful,
perhaps.

43. Along with the evolution of
language — the thousands of
neologisms that new technologies
and new thinking have brought
about, for instance — there has
been a concurrent, if perhaps less
recognizable, devolution of
language. The English language has
become more precise for some users
of it while becoming more plodding
for others. Not a small part of this
179

new cumbrousness is due to the loss of distinctions between words, the misuse of words, and other abuses of language.

44. Swear words are among the least expressive words available to us. They are boring and boorish at once. Using scatological phrases and swear words no longer shocks anyone and suggests only that you are not clever enough to think of better, more meaningful words. Very likely your writing is no more readable than you yourself are companionable.

45. Though sports and even the word *sports* may make us imagine action and excitement, sports metaphors are among our most prosaic expressions. Those who use them are precisely as dull and uninspired as are their words.

46. As the meaning of one word distinguishes it from the meaning of another, so the words we use distinguish each of us from others.

Language, how we express ourselves as much as what we express, is designed to discriminate; it distinguishes, it defines, it identifies. We choose our friends, we choose our work, and we choose our words.

47. Distinguish your writing and speaking from others', and you distinguish yourself.

48. Slang is ephemeral. A slang word popular one year may be forgotten the next. As clever as some slang is, if you use it in your writing, you'll ensure that your writing is equally ephemeral.

49. Since how a person speaks and writes is a fair reflection of how a person thinks and feels, shoddy language may imply a careless and inconsiderate people — a public whose ideals have been discarded and whose ideas have been distorted. And in a society of this sort, easiness and mediocrity are much esteemed.

181

50. The modern prescriptivist is as just in his social and political views as he is exacting in his grammar and usage. Upholding the values of accuracy, clarity, and elegance goes beyond speaking and writing the language well; it also means upholding the values of honesty, grace, and justice.

51. The modern prescriptivist is concerned with speaking and writing well — and with having the language, the usage and grammar, with which to do so.

52. No grace is found in jargon; no compassion in slang. Whenever we express stock sentiments and common vulgarisms, we surrender sincerity and forfeit honesty.

53. The evidence is widespread, even inescapable, that society suffers if people use language sloppily. At the very least, people misunderstand — or may very well misunderstand — each other, which can result in anything from embarrassment to ruin.

54. Worse still is the deliberate misuse of language. We all have suffered from the euphemisms, the circumlocutions, and the unadorned duplicity of businesspeople, politicians, lawyers, and others. With each word of deceit, something is undone: truth and meaning, grace and compassion, society itself.

55. More than incorrect grammar and an infelicitous style, the deliberate misuse of words is an assault on language and society.

56. A society is generally as lax as its language.

57. Let us express ourselves as never before — elegantly, in writing that demands to be read aloud, in speech that calls to be captured in print.

Robert Hartwell Fiske is the editor and publisher *of The Vocabula Review* (vocabula.com). He is the author of *The Dictionary of Unendurable English, To the Point: A Dictionary of Concise Writing, and The Dimwit's Dictionary.*

Vocabula Books Order Form			
Book	Qty	Price	Total
Elegant English		$14.00	
Vocabula Bound 1: Outbursts, Insights, Explanations, and Oddities		$24.95	
Vocabula Bound 2: Our Wresting, Writhing Tongue		$24.95	
Postage and handling [*$5.00 per book in The United States and Canada*]		$5.00	
		Grand Total	

Send your check,
made out to Vocabula Books, to
Vocabula
5A Holbrook Court
Rockport, MA 01966